Helping Children
Hang On To Your Every Word

by
Maggie Johnson

Illustrated by
Robyn Gallow

A QEd Publication

Published in 2007
Reprinted in 2009

ISBN 978 1 898873 53 2

British Library Cataloguing
A catalogue record for this book is available from the British Library.

Published by QEd Publications, 39 Weeping Cross, Stafford ST17 0DG
Tel: 01785 620364
Fax: 01785 607797
Website: www.qed.uk.com
Email: orders@qed.uk.com

Acknowledgement
With thanks to Margaret White for Appendix 5 on page 58.

Printed by Gutenberg Press Ltd, Malta.

Contents

Introduction

Why is it that the children who can least afford to switch off are the ones who don't pay attention? And that children who most need to ask for help are the ones least likely to do so? If children are opting out in the classroom, switching off or passively waiting for direction, we need to understand the barriers they face and help them engage by making their learning opportunities more meaningful, interactive and rewarding.

This book aims to make classroom experience more accessible to all learners, and highlights the links between behaviour and hidden language processing difficulties. Based on tried and tested activities, strategies and self-help skills, you will find ways of improving attention and concentration linked to a simple troubleshooting guide.

Engagement and attention control

Many factors contribute to the level of attention we give to specific tasks at any one time, some positive, some negative. Do we understand what we are meant to be doing and see the point of it? Will we benefit? Do we have the energy to concentrate without distractions or discomfort? Are we enjoying ourselves? Are we in a fit state emotionally to tackle it right now?

Although the answers to these questions will clearly overlap and influence each other, in practice we can identify and consider a number of contributing factors which can be fine-tuned to get the most out of each learning opportunity. These include:

The environment and what we bring to the situation

	Comfort	Freedom from unpleasant physical conditions such as pain, hunger, constraint and extremes of temperature.
	Focus	Having the energy and ability to concentrate on the task in hand.
	Distractions	Anything which takes our attention away from the task in hand.
	Troubles	Personal anxieties, concerns or frustrations. Lack of confidence, self-belief and self-esteem.

The task itself

	Organisation	Being prepared and in control. Knowing exactly what is happening, what is coming up, our involvement and how long it will last.
	Understanding	Making sense of the information we are given and being clear about rules and expectations.

The end-product

	Motivation	How much we want to do something. Dependent on enjoyment and personal gain.
	SuXess Factor	The ability to succeed and willingness to persist until the task is completed.

Each factor or *Attention Control* will vary on a sliding-scale from low to high depending on the time of day, task in hand, preceding events, environmental conditions and so on. In a given situation we will find that some elements are beyond our control – the faulty air-conditioning, the uncomfortable chairs, the incomprehensible speaker! But for every element beyond our control, there will be many more we *can* control to facilitate an enjoyable and effective learning experience. Young children are reliant on adults to consider each control and do the fine-tuning, but as they get older we can involve them in the process and invite their feedback.

Our aim should be for pupils to reach a point where they can identify the stumbling blocks in their learning experience and be equipped with the strategies to surmount these or seek appropriate help.

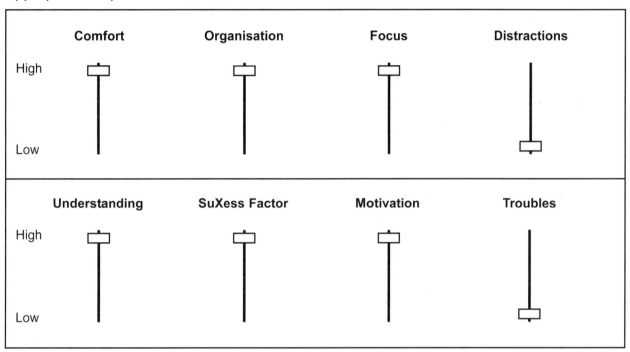

Figure 1: Ideal settings for sustained attention

Figure 1 shows the ideal settings for sustaining attention and getting the maximum out of any learning opportunity, i.e. low interference from physical, sensory and emotional distractions and high ratings on the remaining controls. We will go on to explore ways that staff and pupils can work together to ensure that these settings are maintained in this ideal position. But first of all, in order to appreciate how this model can be used to both understand and address poor attention levels in different situations, it may be useful to apply it to ourselves.

How important is motivation?

We tend to think of enjoyment as a crucial factor in motivation and may find ourselves saying things like: 'He'll do it if he wants to'. Interestingly however, motivation does not have to be high in order to get a job done, and even when it is very high, we cannot always sustain our attention. It is, therefore, presumptuous to conclude that a child has no desire to please adults and is only interested in activities involving Playstations just because this is all he or she seems able to engage in. It is more useful to use the attention controls to ask questions such as:

- **What factors are operating during activities of the child's choosing?**

- **What helps us to see a task through, even when we are not particularly enjoying it?**

- **Can we introduce or increase these factors in other activities to improve enjoyment and hence motivation?**

Applying the model

Three scenarios follow in which motivation is initially high. In each case however, the adult is unable to persevere and disengages. We have a natural sense of why this is and can automatically target the problem areas to improve or remedy the situation.

Scenario 1 – an evening at the theatre

Carol has been looking forward to this play for over a month. It's a Friday night after a busy week and after quite a rush, she arrives at the theatre just in time for the performance. She's feeling pretty tired and ready to switch off for the weekend. Seats are comfy, lights are low, theatre is warm . . . she starts drifting off. She tries to stay awake but it feels like a losing battle. If it wasn't for the irritating rustle of sweets behind her she'd be snoring by the interval.

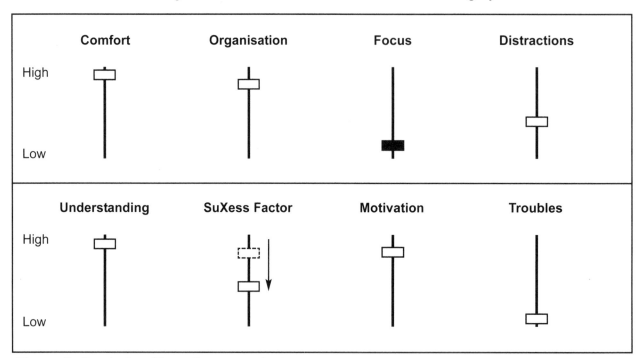

Figure 2: Control settings for scenario 1

Problem

 Focus – static activity with no interaction, low energy.

Carol's solutions

- Move around in seat to try to keep awake.
- Get some fresh air and stretch legs in the interval; avoid wine and go for strong coffee.
- Take water in for second half.
- Next time book a matinee!

What creates similar scenarios in the classroom?

- Poor diet and/or no breakfast.
- Water not freely available.
- Too much listening without physical activity.

Scenario 2 – a study day

Useful course and the agenda looks good so John's motivation is high. Unfortunately it takes place in a hot airless room, backing onto noisy roadworks. The seats are close together and every movement from John's neighbour becomes an extra irritation. He is struggling to hear what the speaker is saying and finding it hard to concentrate in the heat. Fatigue quickly turns to frustration – he decides to grab what handouts he can and leave at lunchtime.

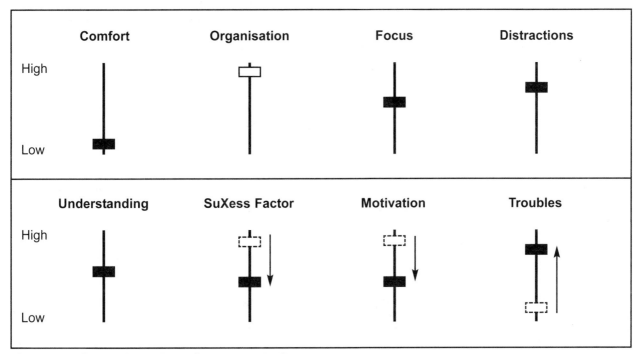

Figure 3: Control settings for scenario 2

Problem

 Comfort – temperature, thirst, cramped conditions.

 Distractions – body discomfort, road drill.

 Focus – too much listening, not enough interaction/movement.

 Understanding – can't hear properly, insufficient visuals to compensate.

Organiser's solutions

- Apologise to participants and compensate with longer breaks or earlier finish.
- Bring in fans and jugs of iced water and microphone for speaker.
- Ensure seats are not too close together. Intersperse listening periods with practical activities.
- Give handouts to delegates in advance and allow some periods for reading and shared reflection.
- Next time blow the budget and book a room with air-conditioning!

What creates similar scenarios in the classroom?

- Children sitting too close together.
- Children unable to monitor own temperature and adjust clothes accordingly.
- Too much listening without visual clues to support understanding.
- Excessive background noise.
- Inability to ignore distractions (sensory processing difficulties).

Scenario 3 – aerobics class

You are determined to get fit and sign up for a fitness class having been assured at the reception desk that you'll cope beautifully. You're not quite so sure so you seek the security of the back row. Within minutes you know you are out of your depth – the rest of the class clearly know all the routines and the instructor is going too fast for you and not breaking the moves down. When she spots you struggling she invites you to come to the front so you can see her better. Eventually you feel less and less like trying and resolve to go to the gym instead.

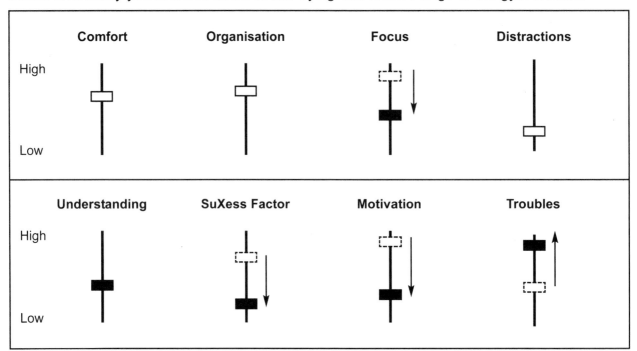

Figure 4: Control settings for scenario 3

Problem

1   **Organisation** – unfamiliar routine so don't know what to expect and can't pace self.

Understanding – not keeping up with instructions, not understanding terms like 'box step' and 'lunge' so reliant on copying others. Can't see well as too self-conscious to go to the front.

Focus – too much to concentrate on at once and tiring with mental effort involved.

Troubles – feel left out, embarrassed, stupid, despondent and frustrated.

Comfort – out of breath . . . but no pain, no gain!

Instructor's solutions

- Welcome new members and invite rest of class to look out for them and help as necessary.
- Explain that newcomers are bound to make mistakes to start with, as did the others, and reassure that after a few weeks it will all fall into place.
- Give an overview of class content with approximate timings.
- Provide two or three options with certain exercises for easy, intermediate and advanced fitness levels.
- Walk down to back occasionally to make positive comments and give a couple of tips.

Your solutions

- Go with a friend – there's strength in numbers.

What produces this effect in the classroom?

- Lack of task-differentiation.
- Assurance that tasks are 'easy' when in fact, for that child, they are difficult.
- Low self-esteem and history of failure leading to lack of self-belief and persistence.
- Poor awareness of time or routine – no notion that the end is in sight.
- Isolation and lack of team identity.

Addressing low motivation

We have seen how outside influences can prevent us from sustaining attention, despite being well-motivated. In the fourth scenario we have the reverse situation where motivation is low but the job still gets done. This helps us to understand *which controls are most significant in overcoming resistance to a task*.

Scenario 4 – attending a meeting

The Annual General Meeting for a local society has come around and Mike knows it will be a tedious affair. Nonetheless he wants to support the group who do a sterling job in the community the rest of the year – it's only once a year after all.

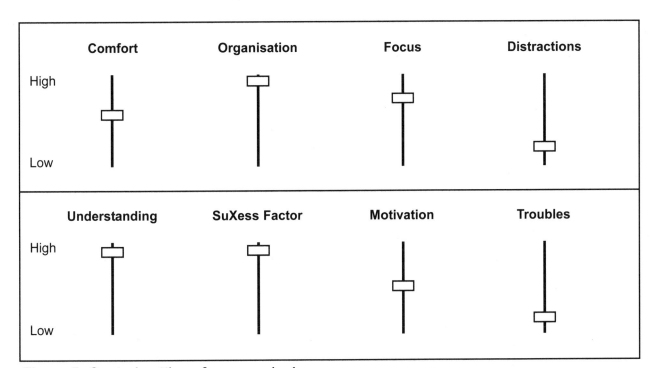

Figure 5: Control settings for scenario 4

Situation and solutions

Motivation – Mike is not enjoying the activity but wants to be seen to be supportive. He knows the committee members value his presence and wishes to maintain their good opinion of him.

Comfort – hard village hall chairs, but no-one complains when Mike shifts in his seat.

Focus – Mike drifts off occasionally but follows the main points and votes at the appropriate moments. Doodling on his agenda helps maintain concentration.

Troubles – Mike knows the task is well within his capability so his only troubles relate to discomfort and disinterest.

Organisation – thanks to good planning, Mike has an agenda and a chairman who keeps the meeting to good time. Ticking off each item brings his planned trip to the pub ever closer and he can see he'll make it well before closing time!

What creates a similar situation in the classroom?

There are many classroom activities that may not be intrinsically interesting, but need to be done. As demonstrated by Scenario 4, the main factors influencing task completion are:

- Good understanding of what is required with a clear endpoint.
- Belief that the task is achievable.
- Positive associations with past experience building motivation to complete task, gain approval and be part of a team.
- Lesson plans and timings that enable pupils to pace themselves.
- Clear overall routine so pupils know what is happening next.
- Appreciation that some movement is essential to maintain comfort and focus.

Taking the pupils' perspective

The above scenarios illustrate how, as adults, we regard our attention to task as a product of task presentation and environmental influences, rather than our own application and attitude to learning. In most cases we put the onus on others to make it easy for us to engage. So it is essential that we ask ourselves the following questions:

- **Do we apply the same reasoning when it comes to children switching off during listening activities?**
- **Do we ask ourselves what is making it difficult for them to listen and target specific areas to remedy the situation, or do we repeatedly entreat them to pay attention and try harder?**

While some children are able to quickly refocus, many are not, and in these cases we need to put ourselves in their shoes and ask how we can make it easier for them to pay attention.

The final scenarios illustrate how the attention controls can be fine-tuned to improve the situation for a child with hidden learning difficulties who is regarded as poorly behaved in the classroom.

Scenario 5a – listening activity

The class is required to listen to a story before the pupils break off into discussion groups to explore character motivation and devise an ending. Darren is seated close to the teacher because he generally fidgets and distracts other children during such activities.

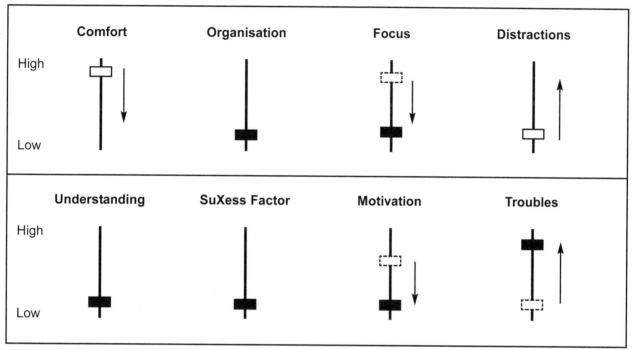

Figure 6: Control settings for scenario 5a

Problem

Understanding and Focus – despite Darren's apparently well-developed speech, he has difficulties processing language at speed and will still be thinking about one sentence as the next is delivered. Words tend to 'wash over him' and quickly lose their meaning. It is very difficult for Darren to maintain attention to something he is not understanding.

Organisation – Darren finds it very difficult to complete work as he is a disorganised thinker and lacks the ability to methodically plan and execute tasks. He was unable to understand the verbal explanation of the task, so lacks a clear internal plan and has no idea how long the session will last. He finds it increasingly difficult to maintain focus and becomes agitated and restless.

Troubles and SuXess Factor – Darren is repeatedly asked to sit still and pay attention and does not like the negative attention this draws to him, alongside the knowledge that he has no idea what he is supposed to be doing and is struggling to keep up with his peers. Darren prefers the attention he gets from entertaining his classmates with silly noises. He relishes the slightest distraction and is actually looking forward to being excluded from the activity so he can sit in the quiet corner away from the spotlight.

Scenario 5b – listening activity with multi-sensory support

The same task is presented with greater emphasis on task breakdown, visual support and active involvement to maintain focus.

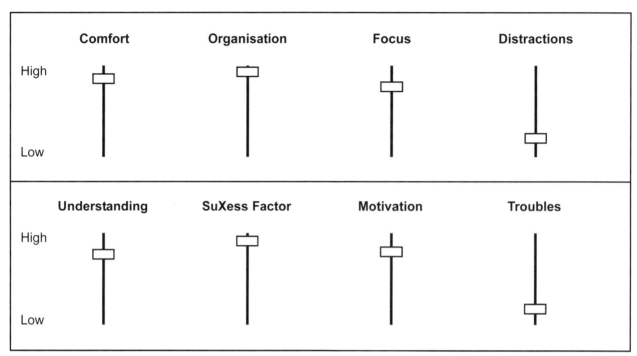

Figure 7: Control settings for scenario 5b

Teacher's Solutions

Organisation – the overall lesson-plan and goal is discussed with the whole class and kept on display during the activity. As each section is completed, a child will be chosen to come to the front and check this off. A clock on the electronic whiteboard shows a countdown of 35 minutes to lunchtime.

Understanding and Focus – as the teacher tells the story the key points and characters are illustrated on the electronic whiteboard. Darren has a worksheet with the same picture sequence and underlines each one as the teacher reaches that point in the story. During the group discussion, the children in Darren's mixed ability group use models representing each character to act out their ideas and allocate roles. Darren is able to see exactly what he needs to do before assuming a character himself and acting out the story-ending.

Comfort – good seating with adequate postural support and personal space. Children know they can move around as long as they do it quietly without invading another child's space.

SuXess Factor – Darren is used to having tasks differentiated so that he can access and participate in the curriculum, so it does not occur to him that he will fail on this occasion.

Motivation – he enjoys the affirmation he gets from his teacher and inclusion in class activities – he often contributes to his group's house-points.

We will now look at each Attention Control in turn and ask the following questions:

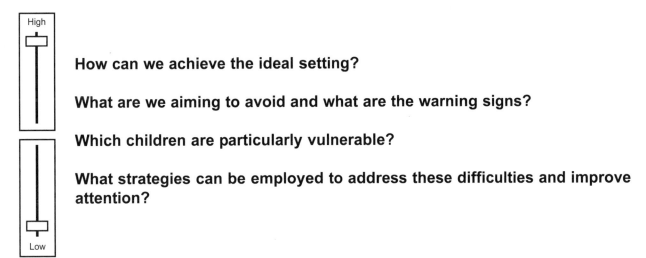

How can we achieve the ideal setting?

What are we aiming to avoid and what are the warning signs?

Which children are particularly vulnerable?

What strategies can be employed to address these difficulties and improve attention?

A framework or 'control panel' is provided to help identify the relevant key areas for particular pupils and tasks, and to troubleshoot possible barriers to sustained attention.

Using the Control Panel

The appendices on pages 79 and 80 provide an Attention Control Panel and prompt sheet which can be photocopied and enlarged, or laminated and used with a dry-wipe marker pen.

The Control Panel sets out the eight attention factors without the sliding controls so that these can be added by an adult or pupil after consideration of the questions on the prompt sheet. Together they can be used in the following ways:

- to create optimum learning conditions when planning a lesson (all teaching stages);
- to introduce the concept of Attention Controls with a group or individual in order for children to gain awareness of their own and others needs (KS2 and above);
- to help students complete their own Attention Control Panel, identify areas for improvement and focus on solutions (KS3 and above).

At first pupils will need help to recognise how they feel and judge where to place the Attention Control. As a general rule of thumb, the mid-position should be selected when:

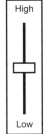

a combination of positive and negative factors are operating, for example, **motivation** – we may not be particularly enjoying a task but have a lot to gain; **comfort** – lovely chairs but slightly chilly, or

things are on the move and deteriorating or improving, for example, **troubles** – frustration rising as can't hear or see properly.

A useful exercise

It may be helpful for older pupils to first consider the control settings for activities they enjoy. Almost without exception, they will arrive at a picture very close to the ideal settings on pages 5 and 12.

Scenario 6 – Playstation, surfing the internet, IPod, watching DVDs

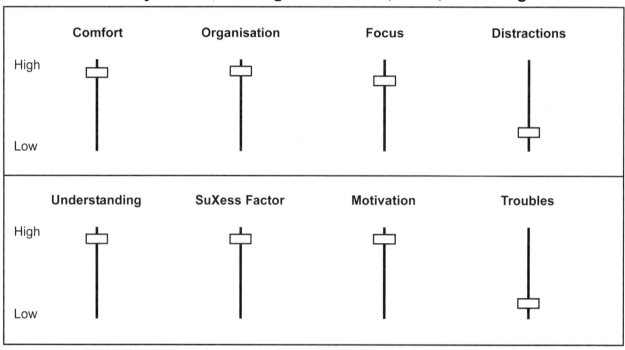

Figure 8: Control settings for scenario 6 (activities of pupils' choosing)

With help, they may then be able to identify the key factors to enjoyment, drive and success in these and other activities:

1   **Organisation** – clear understanding of task with clear end-point, step-by-step consistent rules.

Understanding – visual presentation (which compensates for any language or auditory processing difficulties). New instructions are built on familiar experience and well-established foundations.

Focus – single point of focus, multi-sensory experience (rather than multi-tasking) – keeps brain alert.

Distractions – complete absorption in task puts pupil in cocoon-mode, shutting out all other distractions (unfortunately they may not notice you talking to them either . . .).

SuXess Factor – success is not dependent on language, literacy or memory skills. Past experience leads pupil to expect success, so task is tackled with confidence and persistence.

The remaining sections provide a detailed breakdown of factors important to each area of Attention Control, together with compensatory strategies to support both whole class teaching and individual pupils.

The majority of strategies have an application for learners of all ages and teachers are invited to select materials and opportunities as appropriate to pre-school, primary and secondary school settings. A few strategies are particularly relevant to secondary schools however, and these are highlighted with the symbol [Sec] .

Attention Controls . . . . . Comfort

Am I *comfortable* before I start?

Comfortable

Uncomfortable

Signs that discomfort may be affecting attention span include:

- Increased restlessness, aggressive outbursts.
- Better attention in some positions (e.g. on chair, in beanbag, standing, lying on floor) than others (e.g. sitting on floor, bench or stool).
- Slumping on desks or other children.
- Flushed face and damp hair from excessive sweating.
- Screwing up eyes, blinking.
- Hands over ears.

Low

Factors that are important for comfort include:

- Good balance – stable seating with back and foot support.
- Good view without craning neck or twisting body.
- Freedom to shift weight and avoid soreness/numbness.
- Personal space – not touching other people.
- Good lighting – no glare.
- Sound at an adequate level without interference or feedback.
- Loose non-irritating clothing.
- Temperature of 65-75 degrees F (18-25 degrees C).
- Empty bladder/bowels.
- Satisfied hunger/thirst.

High

Possible barriers within *school* include:

- Over-crowded classrooms.
- Lack of flexibility with class rules (e.g. 'sit still', 'sit up straight', 'don't lean').
- Standard furniture without height adjustment.
- Expectation to sit on floor or benches for long periods of time.
- Drinking water not freely available.

Possible barriers within *pupils* include:

- Inability to attend to content of lessons when struggling to maintain posture or ignore close proximity of other children.
- Poor posture linked to poor balance, body awareness or body-tone. Problematic for pupils with poor physical co-ordination or sensory-integration, including pupils with a diagnosis of developmental co-ordination disorder or 'dyspraxia'. These children can feel very insecure in their seating position and frequently shift position, touch their surroundings or slump.
- Low tolerance to uninvited or unexpected touch/movement (e.g. children with autistic spectrum difficulties or sensory dysfunction).
- Over-sensitivity to sound, light (including glare from the page) and the feel of items such as wet paint, clay or man-made fibres can cause actual discomfort and distress.
- Lack of awareness of need to go to toilet or inability to ask to be excused. Fear of teasing from peers if they go to the toilet
- Lack of awareness of body temperature or pain, and inability to self-regulate.
- Hunger/thirst.

How to improve attention by increasing comfort

Seating

- Help children respect each other's need for personal space and try to ensure there is always space between them when sitting or standing (see also 'Social rules' on page 35).
- Ensure pupils can support their backs by leaning backwards against a surface or forwards on their elbows.
- Feet should be supported in front of body, not at sides or underneath.
- Match furniture to child rather than the other way round. Have adjustable legs on tables/chairs or access to a choice of furniture so feet are flat on floor and table is at elbow height.
- ⟨Sec⟩ Provide foot-rest under bench when using stools.
- Show children how to sit on floor with crossed feet rather than crossed legs. Knees are brought up allowing elbows to rest against them for back support, and hands can be clasped.
- Give 'floppy' pupils a rest by letting them use beanbags, lie on floor or lean on wall/furniture.
- Position touch-sensitive pupils at beginning/end of queues and rows so they have less jostling to contend with.
- Position children in horseshoe formation around tables so all are facing the front without turning.
- See appendix 14 'Listening and attention' on page 71 to match attention levels with appropriate postural support.

Environment

- Check for adequate lighting, comfortable temperature, access to drinking water and pupil's eating pattern.
- Ensure speaker's face is easily visible and well-lit – do not stand in front of window or move out of view while talking.

- Avoid harsh strip-lighting and go for bulbs which simulate daylight.
- Try pastel coloured paper or coloured acetate overlays to see if pupil's reading improves (may be suffering from glare from white paper).
- Encourage pupils to remove outer-clothing when over-heating (may need to calmly explain options/give adequate warning if they are reluctant to change or worried about losing belongings).
- Heed warning signs of distress/discomfort – fingers in ears, hands over eyes, blinking, excessive fidgeting etc. and remove source of agitation.
- Ensure pupil is using toilet at appropriate times (some have a toilet phobia – see 'Troubles' on page 45) and that visits are timetabled for pupils who are unable to anticipate needs. Consider a signing-out system where pupils can excuse themselves without asking, but put their name by a toilet symbol on wall to indicate where they have gone.
- [Sec] Explore possibility that peer pressure is preventing pupils using toilets and ensure privacy is respected.

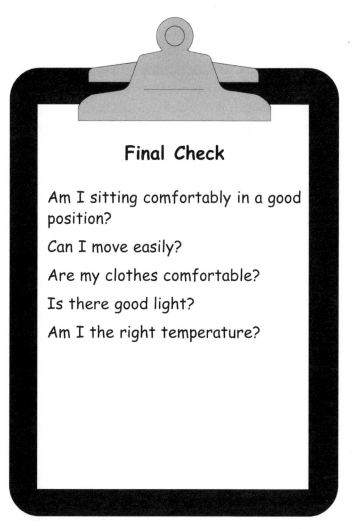

Final Check

Am I sitting comfortably in a good position?

Can I move easily?

Are my clothes comfortable?

Is there good light?

Am I the right temperature?

Useful resources

Social Skills Posters – *Good Sitting* from Taskmaster Ltd, Morris Road, Leicester LE2 6BR (Tel: 0116 270 4286; www.taskmasteronline.co.uk).

Mov'n'Sit cushion from Epsan Waterfly (UK) Ltd (Tel: 01299 829213; www.epsanwaterfly.com)

Aron, E. (2003) *The Highly Sensitive Child: Helping our children thrive when the world overwhelms them.* London: HarperCollins.

Attention Controls . . . . . Organisation

1

> Do I know what's happening now, what's coming up and how long it will take?

Very clear

Very confused

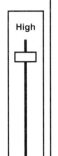

Low

Signs that poor organisation may be affecting attention span include:

- Haphazard approach – works through books or worksheets backwards, misses out pages, deals cards out of sequence.
- Does not work consistently from left to right.
- Repetitive questioning, 'What are we doing?', 'What's next?'
- Good ideas but inability to get started or plan methodically (e.g. stories, design and technology projects).
- Cannot decide what to do first when given several instructions.
- Poor time-management.
- Often in wrong place at the wrong time with the wrong equipment.
- Difficulty generating a mind map without assistance, but benefits from the structure of main and sub-themes.
- Written work and home assignments do not live up to the promise shown in classroom discussion.
- Preference for set routines and easily thrown by change.
- Over-compensation by listing and cataloguing information.

High

Factors that are important for feeling organised and in control include:

- Natural sense of time – an overview of how each task fits into the day, each day fits into the week.
- Arriving on time.
- Good preparation.
- A clear goal for each task and a step-by-step plan for achieving that goal.
- Ability to prioritise.
- Knowing when each task or activity will finish – can then pace self and keep going until the next break.
- Ability to cope with the unexpected.

Possible barriers within *school* include:

- Reduction of support at secondary level where the disorganised student faces an even greater challenge.
- Large sprawling buildings and long corridors without clear landmarks.
- Open-plan classrooms with regular changes in seating arrangements and layout.
- Timetables with the days of the week running across the top rather than down the side.
- 'Busy' whiteboards and worksheets packed with information.
- Lack of time/manpower to differentiate tasks, prepare detailed work plans and reminder systems, and assist with study skills.

Possible barriers within *child* include:

- Problems with visuo-spatial perception (our ability to process and interpret visual information about where objects are in space) associated with poor body-awareness, co-ordination difficulties, comprehension or social-communication difficulties. This makes it difficult to quickly and methodically sift text, images and objects for patterns, groups and key information.
- Scanning and focusing difficulties – difficulty working from the centre of the page outwards; tracking a moving person or object and copying from the board.
- Poor inferencing skills – cannot work out steps that are implied or assumed.
- Inflexibility and rigidity of thought (e.g. ASD and Asperger's Syndrome) leading to inability to plan for or cope with the unexpected; difficulty relating to the concept 'it depends' and a pervasive insecurity about what lies around the next corner.
- Impaired executive functioning or more simply, disorganisation! This results in impulsivity and difficulty initiating, planning and shifting between activities.
- Poor analytical skills – difficulty breaking tasks down into smaller components.
- Poor time-concept – relates to here and now rather than projecting into future or reviewing past. Difficulty establishing routines, pacing self and anticipating events.

How to improve attention by compensating for pupil's poor organisational skills

Clear information

- Teach methodical scanning, working from left to right and top to bottom in a variety of tabletop and floor activities. Consistent layout will give disorganised children a reliable base from which they can later scan and process text, tables, timelines and worksheets.
- Use visual markers and arrows to highlight the top-left starting point and direction of text/information. A good rule of thumb for time sequences is to set out daily events and story sequences from left to right, and a breakdown of steps within the same task or event from top to bottom.
- Keep worksheets and the whiteboard uncluttered, setting out information in clearly demarcated boxes, columns and rows.
- Use bullet-points, lists, index cards and flow-charts for recording, accessing and memorising information. Use colour to box and highlight key information.
- Disorganised children tend to process information most efficiently when working from the top of the page rather than the centre (as do visually impaired pupils). If they find the free-flowing layout of mind maps difficult to work with, use a linear layout (see appendix 6 on page 59 for examples, or the Kidspiration Software*).

Being on a mission

- Encourage independent working and ability to seek help by providing a work-plan with step-by-step instructions which pupils can refer to, check off as they go and use to identify where they get stuck. Always include an overview of the task goal/end product and timescale (see appendices on pages 54 to 57 for sample frameworks and lesson plans).
- Once familiar with this way of working, help children create and use their own 'To Do' lists.
- Forward planning, good preparation and liaison with support staff will be vital to transmitting a sense of purpose and focus to pupils. Share lesson objectives and learning points with the whole class within an overview of the topic. Provide a written summary for support staff to share with individual pupils (see appendix 4 on page 57 for an example).
- Ensure tasks can be finished within the time allowed, and that pupils know how long they have got. Use sand-timers, clocks, stop-watches, checklists and 'Time Timers' (see resources) as appropriate so that children can pace themselves and concentrate for the duration.
- Set tasks with a clear end-point and finish when the buzzer (real or metaphorical) goes. By continually saying 'Just one more' or 'A couple more minutes' children do not learn to pace themselves, estimate time or have a sense of task-completion.

Being on time

- Recognise that being on time is as difficult for disorganised children as breaking the alphabetic code is for poor-readers. They need support and compensatory strategies rather than disapproval.
- Give child an alarm/timer at break/lunchtime if they are constantly side-tracked and late or pair them up with a reliable time-keeper. Show older children how to set the alarm on a watch or mobile phone.
- If time is an issue, use friends to collect or accompany children rather than leaving them to find their own way.
- Help children find their way around the school by colour-coding different areas with coloured lines to follow on floor or along walls.
- Help children to 'do a recce' whenever possible and practise going over a route beforehand at a quiet time, e.g. during classtime when the corridors are clear.
- Give a five minute warning before starting and finishing activities and make this visual with 5-4-3-2-1 on whiteboard or cards.
- Establish and practise class rules for change-over times. Changing from one activity to another needs to be quick and quiet (especially when moving chairs) and involves clearing the last activity before moving to, or getting ready for the next. If tidying up is taking too long, give the class 'five' to be in position and count up to five while they move quickly and quietly. Nominate two 'helping hands' each week to finish putting away and pushing chairs in so that only two are busy and the rest of the class are ready quickly.
- Recognise that we all need time to settle rather than launching into tasks immediately on arrival. Establish a routine so that children know exactly what to do when they come into class and are waiting for lessons to start. Allow latecomers the same time to settle by getting other children to summarise the lesson so far, and deal with the issue of being on time on a separate occasion.

Personal organisation

- Help child keep desk as uncluttered as possible by developing good habits of 'Get everything you need' and 'Put away everything you don't need' before each task.
- Give lots of help to get organised before task so that child has a better chance of completing task independently.
- Provide different coloured folders for different topics.
- Secure items on the desk using blutak, central container, weights etc.
- Don't berate children who keep losing pencils, pens, or other supplies. Provide an extra supply (perhaps parents can help out?) so children can help themselves without having to go around trying to borrow supplies or interrupting the lesson.
- Build in a weekly time for clearing out desks, trays and bags or it will become too overwhelming a task for the child.
- Put important reminders in a homework diary or school-home book – and ensure child looks at it before they go home. This may involve a routine check with a classroom assistant or class buddy for younger children, or an agreed signal or reminder for older children (e.g. a sticker on their coat-peg or inside their locker).
- Use the Reminder menu on mobile phones to set off an alarm at home with a reminder to bring swimming bag, packed lunch etc.
- Is there something the child **never** leaves the house without? If so, put it with whatever they need to remember to take to school the next day (this works for adults too!).
- Put days of the week down the side (not across the top) of personal timetables.

Feeling in control

- Routine is very important for security, anticipation and adaptation. Adopt a basic routine and set this out pictorially left to right so children can be reminded of where they are in the day. Symbols are usually quicker to use than pictures (e.g. Widget Symbols 2000).

- Help establish the concept of time-passing by encouraging children to colour in or check off completed activities or events. This maintains an overall sense of time as the child can still see all the things they have done, as well as what's coming up.
- Prepare children for changes in routine by swapping pictures around or inserting new ones, and forewarn children of any loud noises before they occur. Make quick changes with Post-it notes.
- Take a section of the basic routine and break it down into smaller steps if necessary, e.g. changing for PE, lunchtime routine, assembly.
- Introduce an empty 'surprise' box into the pictorial timetable on some days, so that children can cope with waiting until later in the day to find out what they will be doing. Then, when something unexpected occurs, reassure anxious children by calling it a 'surprise'. Draw a picture of it and add it to their timetable so that they can see that nothing else needs to change as a result.

- See Timelines on page 59 for visual frameworks to support daily routine.
- At end of the day, look at the pictorial timetable with the class or individual children and review what the children have done. Pick out their favourite bits and best achievements so they can tell parents. Now look briefly at what's coming up the following day.
- Ask parents to do the same at the end of the weekend and school holidays, so that children come into school with some key points for their news and are prepared for the change in routine.
- Disorganised children will do better working with a digital rather than analogue clock-face. Apart from teaching o'clock and half-past, it is easier to establish the overall concept of the passage of time using digital continuity, returning to analogue clocks later.
- Encourage independent working and ability to seek help by providing a work-plan with step-by-step instructions which pupils can refer to, check off as they go and use to identify where they get stuck.
- Ensure pupils are able to seek clarification *when* they get stuck rather than *if* they get stuck. See appendix 7 'What is an active listener?' on page 63.
- Check that channels for seeking information are made explicit and that pupils are familiar with the sources of information available to them.

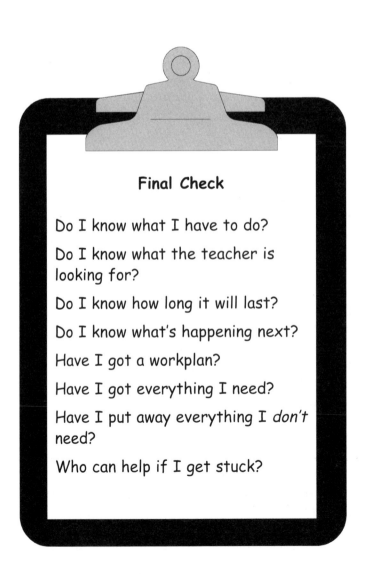

Final Check

Do I know what I have to do?

Do I know what the teacher is looking for?

Do I know how long it will last?

Do I know what's happening next?

Have I got a workplan?

Have I got everything I need?

Have I put away everything I *don't* need?

Who can help if I get stuck?

Useful resources

Kidspiration Software Package, Inspiration Software, Inc., 9400 SW Beaverton-Hillsdale Hwy, Suite 300, Beaverton, OR 97005-3300 www.inspiration.com

Social Skills Posters: *Good Asking* (personal organisation) from Taskmaster Ltd, Morris Road, Leicester LE2 6BR (Tel: 0116 270 4286; www.taskmasteronline.co.uk).

Johnson, M. (2005) *Functional Language In the Classroom* (coping strategies for organisation). Manchester Metropolitan University Commercial Office, 0161 247 2535.

Writing with Symbols 2000 from Widgit Software Ltd, 124 Cambridge Science Park, Milton Rd, Cambridge CB4 0ZS (Tel: 01223 425 558; www.widgit.com).

Johnson, M. and Player, C. (2009) *Active Listening for Active Learning* from QEd Publications, Stafford ST17 0DG (Tel: 01785 620 364; www.qed.uk.com).

Attention Controls . . . . . Focus

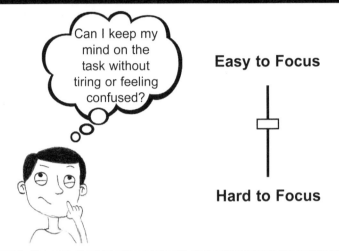

Easy to Focus

Hard to Focus

Low

Signs that poor focus may be affecting attention span include:

- Good attention for single-channel activities (e.g. computer, video) but difficulty concentrating on different things and places at the same time (e.g. teacher's voice, whiteboard and worksheet).
- Better attention one-to-one than in group activities.
- Inability to settle to or complete task.
- Attending to only one part of the task.
- Yawning, lethargy.
- Despondency, irritability, aggression.
- Seeking out distractions.
- Chewing cuffs and collars.
- Hyperactivity.

High

Factors that are important for focus include:

- Maintaining energy levels with an adequate diet, good hydration and plenty of sleep.
- Changing activity at regular intervals and taking regular breaks.
- Use of complementary movement, touch, action and/or visuals to keep activities multi-sensory.
- Keeping the number of things that simultaneously require our attention to a minimum.
- Recognising our limitations and avoiding overload.
- Freedom to unobtrusively fidget/doodle/touch/move ('keeps the brain awake').
- Freedom from discomfort, distractions and anxiety.

Possible barriers within *school* include:

- Open-plan classrooms which require children to turn to whiteboard and keep track of a moving adult – while listening to instructions and looking at workbooks.
- Emphasis on copying from whiteboard can deplete energy and reduce application for more relevant aspects of task.
- Lack of flexibility with class rules (e.g. 'hands still', 'put pens down', 'no fidgeting').
- Drinking water not freely available.
- Lack of time/manpower to adequately differentiate tasks and work in smaller groups.

Possible barriers within a *child* include:

- Language comprehension or processing difficulties make it impossible to attend to the spoken word unless there is a visual focus (e.g. TV, puppet show, storybook).
- Social-communication difficulties (poor understanding of social behaviour and rules) require children to concentrate on the rules of listening, turn-taking, sharing and team-working in addition to the task in hand.
- Poor posture or balance requires children to concentrate as much on sitting on chair as on main activity.
- Learning difficulties cause children to fatigue easily – they require extra effort to process information and are easily overloaded.
- Poorly developed attention (part of an overall delay or specific disorder such as ADHD) means children will:
  - find it difficult or impossible to focus on more than one thing at a time;
  - have a very short attention span unless highly motivated or involved in a single-channel activity with visual/kinaesthetic input (for example, computers/Gameboy/gardening/sports etc.);
  - try to increase their focus by repetitive movements like tapping, fiddling or chewing.
- Poor 'auditory figure-ground perception' – an inability to separate the main sound (e.g. teacher's voice) from background noise.
- Poor 'visual figure-ground perception' – an inability to separate the main image from the background (e.g. patterned border, elaborate mindmap, cluttered whiteboard).
- Poor diet, or no time for breakfast.
- Abstinence from food/drink as afraid to ask for or use the toilet.

How to improve attention by increasing pupil's ability to focus

Variety

- Provide a variety of activity and pace with a balance of listening/looking/doing activities. Build in frequent changes and learning breaks with the opportunity to move, even if this just means swapping activity stations in the classroom.
- Intersperse listening sessions with opportunities for discussion/reflection/practice in small groups.
- Address class from different places in the room, but talk – move – stand still – talk. Do not talk while constantly on the move.
- Stop for a movement song or action rhyme if session is making children restless. Get children to jump up to 'shake their sillies out', do a couple of Brain Gym or Write Dance activities, or run round the playground. Let individuals bounce on a trampette or run an errand.
- Allow quiet fiddling (blutak/stress ball etc) which does not distract others.
- Sec Allow doodling during listening activities.
- Find something more appropriate for children to chew than their clothes or pencils, e.g. a hard pencil top or 'chewy-tube'.

Warning

- Give a five minute warning before starting and finishing activities and make this visual with 5–4–3–2–1 on whiteboard or cards.
- Gain pupils attention before you speak with their name or a general class request. Find an age-appropriate routine and stick to it, and do not start talking again until everyone is listening. For example:
    - say 'let me see empty hands' so that children stop what they are doing and wave hands or wiggle fingers in the air to show they are listening;
    - hold up hand, say 'Stop and Listen', then count down 5–4–3–2–1 on fingers, counting aloud and encouraging children to join in;
    - do this in silence to achieve calm. Count down from 5 only using fingers, then put fingers on lips until all class have stopped talking and are doing the same;
    - if tidying up the workspace is taking too long, say 'You have five to . . .' (e.g. be on the carpet/line up at the door) and count up to five, having nominated two 'helping-hands' to finish tidying up, push chairs in etc.;
    - get children to copy your actions until all the class have joined in. Wiggle your fingers, then change and tap your head, tap your shoulders, stick out your tongue etc. When all the children have caught on, fold your arms;
    - stand next to a table and quietly say 'clap once if you can hear me' then 'clap twice if you can hear me', until all the class have caught on;
    - say 'stop and rest' as a cue to stop what they are doing and fold their arms;
    - agree a word of the week (may be linked to topic). For example: 'This week if you hear me say "fireworks" then you have to stop and put your hands in the air'.
- Ensure a TA or sensible child is positioned to give an individual reminder to children who find it difficult to switch their focus of attention (see Developmental Progression for listening and attention on page 71 [part of SuXess module]).

Energy

- Use pupils' own interests to heighten motivation and focus in lessons/assignments.
- Provide access to water/fresh air. Spot low energy points of day and consider introducing biscuits/crackers/fruit.
- Breakfast clubs.
- Watch for pupils who are not eating/drinking (see 'Troubles' on page 45).
- Keep children focused by mirroring/affirming their response followed by your interpretation – 'What I think you're trying to say is . . .'.
- Notice when pupils are doing well – 'Great, keep that up'.

Reduce overload

- Reduce multi-tasking activities and increase use of multi-sensory single-channel activities if pupil is prone to overload (see chart on next page for examples).
- Avoid focusing on two skills at the same time when neither is well-established, e.g. turn-taking and topic vocabulary (see 'Understanding' on page 33 for rules on sharing, listening and turn-taking).
- Quick-fix for poor balance – pupils may concentrate better if standing or leaning.
- Flexible class rules: ASD pupils find it very uncomfortable and off-putting to watch speaker's face while listening/processing information. All children should face speaker however. When eye contact is difficult, pupils may need to indicate they are listening by turning one ear to you, folding their arms etc.
- Reduce unnecessary interference (see 'Distractions' on page 30).
- Less talk, more action! Back up spoken language with visual support – the whole class will benefit! (see appendix 9 for visual and kinaesthetic learners on page 65).

Learning Channel	Examples of single-channel activities	Examples of single-channel, multi-sensory activities	Examples of multi-channel, activities (multi-tasking)
Conversation	Answering questions about weekend activities.	Discussing a topic with a shared focal point e.g. holiday photos or piece of music; answering questions with picture clues to support understanding.	Talking about the weekend while making a glove puppet; playing I-Spy while remembering to articulate sounds correctly.
Reading	Reading aloud to teaching assistant (TA).	Reading aloud while TA uses cued articulation* prompts; matching two halves of a sentence together – both symbols* and words on cards.	Reading aloud while TA interjects and asks questions about the pictures or text; completing a questionnaire while watching TV.
Wring/Drawing	Copying. Colouring.	Filling in a worksheet with music in the background; writing a story using a writing frame for structure and content.	Filling in a worksheet while watching a science experiment and listening to teacher; copying from the whiteboard.
Look/Select	Pick out all the blue marbles.	Playing a computer game, working keyboard and calling out score; moving interactive images on whiteboard; jigsaw puzzle.	Playing a computer game while explaining to someone how it works; threading beads in repeated colour sequence.
Listening	Lying on floor listening to a story.	Listening to chef giving a cookery demonstration; listening to music and counting the number of cymbal crashes; listening to a story sitting on floor in uncomfortable position.	Playing football and listening to coach calling out instructions from sideline; listening to classroom instructions while still engrossed in painting; listening to a story tape, stopping at bell, writing down answer, turning page and restarting tape.
Thinking/Reasoning	Riddles. Noughts and crosses.	Sorting topic vocabulary cards into different categories; working out shopping list needed for camping trip while discussing plans in a group.	Working out shopping list needed for camping trip while rest of group ask what clothes you'll be packing; trying to follow timetable while remembering to scan it top to bottom.
Action	Follow my leader. Making paper chains.	Action-Rhymes; acting out a familiar story; using own bodies to emulate an electrical circuit with switches and current.	Improvising a role-play scenario; putting up a tent, following instruction manual and allocating tasks.

*See Useful resources on next page

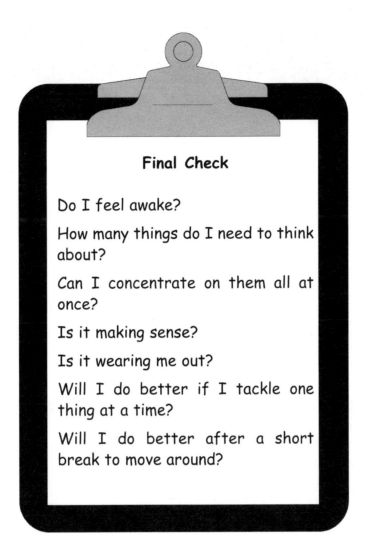

Final Check

Do I feel awake?

How many things do I need to think about?

Can I concentrate on them all at once?

Is it making sense?

Is it wearing me out?

Will I do better if I tackle one thing at a time?

Will I do better after a short break to move around?

Useful resources

Chewy Tubes from Kapitex Healthcare Ltd, Kapitex House, 1 Sandbeck Way, Wetherby, West Yorkshire LS22 7GH (Tel: 01937 580211).

Brain Gym from Educational Kinesiology UK Foundation, 12, Golders Rise, London NW4 2HR (Tel: 020 8202 3141; www.braingym.org.uk).

Oussoren Voors, R. (2000) *Write Dance: A Progressive Music and Movement Programme for the Development of Pre-writing and Writing Skills in Children*. Bristol: Lucky Duck Publishers.

Passy J. (1993) *Cued Articulation*. Ponteland: STASS Publications. (Tel: 01661 822 316).

Writing with Symbols 2000 from Widgit Software Ltd, 124 Cambridge Science Park, Milton Rd, Cambridge CB4 0ZS (Tel: 01223 425 558; www.widgit.com).

Attention Controls . . . . . Distractions

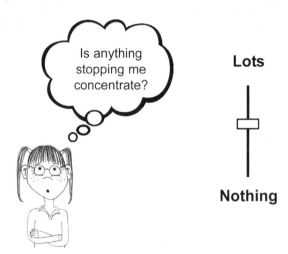

Lots

Nothing

High

Signs that distractions may be affecting attention span include:
- Inability to settle to task.
- Inability to complete task.
- Getting side-tracked when running errands.
- Forgetting job in hand.
- Turning to every sound, movement etc.

Low

Factors that are important for ignoring distractions include:
- Being on a mission – having a clear sense of purpose and the job that needs to be done.
- Personal space – uncluttered desk, not touching other people, separate rather than overlapping workspace.
- Good view or access without unnecessary detours.
- Tactile stimulation (something to fiddle with, chew or suck).
- Functionality – a place for everything and everything in its place until needed.

Possible barriers within *school* include:
- Over-crowded and cluttered classrooms.
- Lack of flexibility with class rules (e.g. 'hands still', 'put pens down').
- Insufficient space for quiet, plainly decorated corners away from distractions.

Possible barriers within *pupils* include:

- Difficulty focusing on, understanding or processing language makes listening a tiring, unfulfilling process. Children are then extremely susceptible to distractions.
- Poor organisation and a lack of purposeful activity reduce confidence and motivation and increase distractibility.
- Immature attention mechanism – 'stimulus-bound'. An inability to prioritise and respond to important information whilst filtering out and ignoring the rest. Consequently the child gives equal weight to all noise and distractions (e.g. teacher's voice, coughing, children moving, footsteps in corridor).
- Lack of body awareness causing a 'floating' sensation as child cannot automatically sense where their limbs are in space. Problematic for pupils with poor sensory-integration, including pupils with a diagnosis of developmental co-ordination disorder or 'dyspraxia'. These children need to touch their surroundings to give them an 'anchor'. This looks like self-distraction but is actually a coping strategy.
- Low tolerance to uninvited or unexpected touch/movement (e.g. children with autistic spectrum difficulties or sensory dysfunction).
- Anxieties (e.g. 'Who's going to pick me up today?') may be playing on mind and not addressed.

How to improve attention by reducing distractions and distractibility

Workspace

- Some children work better with continuous background noise (e.g. music) as this blocks out the unpredictable noise which keeps distracting them.
- Others need total quiet – ask children their preferences and see what options are open to them (e.g. work in library).
- Provide a 'good work' table in quiet or screened-off corner where children can ask to work if they want to get something finished. Distractible children can then be seated there without stigma to help them focus and finish a task.
- Ensure there is sufficient space between children and minimise overlap by providing each with own rubber, ruler etc.
- Provide clear rules for sharing – 'if something is in another child's space you need to ask, not take'.

Focus

- Allow quiet fiddling (Blutak/stress ball etc) which doesn't distract others.
- Use pupils' own interests to heighten motivation and reduce distractibility in lessons/assignments.
- Don't allow self to be side-tracked when pupils go off at a tangent. Refocus them on the question/task in hand but recognise that they went off-topic for a reason – give clarification.

- Keep children focused by noticing when they are doing well.
- Recognise when children need to get things off their chests before settling – e.g. sharing good news, having some quiet time to get over a playground dispute.
- See 'Understanding' (page 33) and 'Organisation' (page 18) to ensure the pupils are engaged and 'on a mission'.

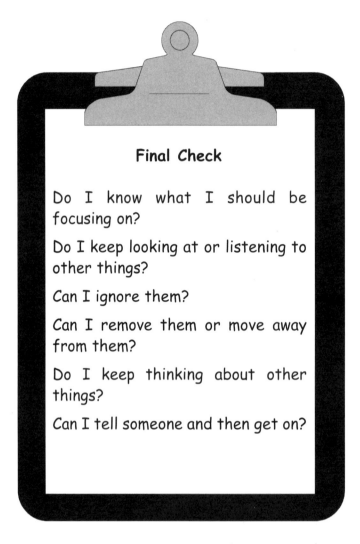

Final Check

Do I know what I should be focusing on?

Do I keep looking at or listening to other things?

Can I ignore them?

Can I remove them or move away from them?

Do I keep thinking about other things?

Can I tell someone and then get on?

Attention Controls . . . . . Understanding

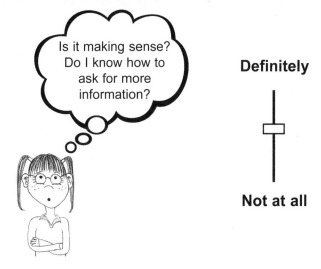

Definitely

Not at all

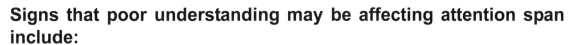

Low

Signs that poor understanding may be affecting attention span include:

- Noticeably better attention one-to-one than in group activities.
- Better attention for practical activities than listening activities.
- Difficulty following verbal instructions but quickly understands from demonstration.
- Reading accuracy better than reading comprehension.
- Starts yawning as soon as required to listen.
- Inappropriate answers and frequent guessing.
- Literal interpretation.
- Repetitive questioning, not processing answer.
- Responds to only part of question.
- Latches on to keywords and responds by association rather than full understanding.
- Speaks fluently with familiar or rote-learnt language, but struggles to reason and explain
- Despondency, irritability, aggression.
- Seeking out distractions, playing the clown.
- Naïve, easily led.

High

Factors that are important for understanding the spoken word include:

- Adequate hearing and sight.
- Good view of teacher, whiteboard and any equipment.
- Good delivery – adequate volume and pace, expressive intonation, careful use of pausing and repetition.
- Visual references to support new concepts, aid visualisation and maintain brain activity.
- Opportunity to reflect and double-check understanding.
- Ability to seek clarification in an appropriate way (active listening).
- A culture where active listening is expected and encouraged rather than simply permitted or invited.

Possible barriers within *school* include:

- Lack of awareness:
  - poor attention may be put down to low effort or motivation rather than poor understanding, particularly if child is able to speak fluently;
  - inappropriate answers may be put down to silliness or poor attention rather than poor understanding.

  Use checklist on page 67 to analyse reasons for inappropriate answers.
- TAs may have more specialist training than the teachers they support. This places TAs in a difficult position unless they are working collaboratively with the teacher or can look to their SENCO or senior management to influence classroom practice.
- Open-plan classrooms with many distractions which make it even harder to focus on the spoken word.
- Lack of time/manpower to adequately differentiate tasks, work in smaller groups, isolate and teach topic vocabulary in advance, liaise with parents regarding homework assignments and give individual assistance as needed both in and outside the classroom.
- Tendency to over-anticipate pupils' needs and give clarification rather than helping pupils develop active listening skills and other self-help strategies.

Possible barriers within *child* include:

- Poor or fluctuating hearing.
- Comprehension difficulties are often accompanied by poor organisation and visuo-spatial or scanning problems (see 'Organisation' on page 18).
- Poor active listening skills go hand in hand with poor comprehension so children are unable to compensate for their lack of understanding by asking for repetition or clarification. Older children may be too embarrassed to ask questions in front of their peers for fear of looking stupid.
- Language comprehension difficulties may be masked by fluent speech (semantic and pragmatic language disorders, social-communication difficulties). These children cannot attend to the spoken word unless there is a visual focus (e.g. picture, worksheet, interactive whiteboard).
- Language may appear to be well-developed when assessed under test conditions, but child may be unable to process continuous language at speed – this often goes hand in hand with literacy problems.
- Social-communication difficulties may prevent children grasping rules of social behaviour and classroom conduct without explicit explanation and practice.
- Poor inferencing skills mean that children understand only what is immediately in front of them and cannot follow indirect reasoning or implied speech such as, 'I don't think Gordon's all that impressed' (i.e. stop tormenting the guinea pig).
- Poor phonological awareness and speech discrimination skills lead to difficulty separating familiar and unfamiliar words in connected speech – overall meaning is compromised and new vocabulary is slow to develop.
- Expressive language difficulties and literacy problems are usually associated with a poor short-term memory for verbal explanations and instructions.
- When extra effort is required to listen and comprehend the result is overload, fatigue and poor concentration – but when pupils are unable to explain or negotiate, this often presents as boredom, lack of motivation or laziness.

- When difficulties go unrecognised, children feel increasingly anxious, useless, frustrated and despondent. They develop a range of opt-out or self-preservation strategies: 'My tummy hurts'; 'Can I go to the toilet?'; 'That's boring, I didn't want to do it anyway'.
- Negative behaviours do not win the pupils any favours and their behaviour and self-esteem are caught in a downward spiral, increasing the likelihood of truancy, school avoidance or exclusion.

How to improve attention by increasing pupil's ability to understand and access the curriculum

Visual input

- Remember that language 'washes over' pupils with poor understanding unless the key points are simultaneously illustrated with visual images and demonstration or experienced through action. In this respect they are like all visual and kinaesthetic learners – their strengths lie in processing, memorising and recalling information through images, touch and action rather than language alone (see appendix 9 'Less talk, more action!' on page 65 for ways to cater for their learning style).
- Back up verbal explanations and instructions with visual information to help maintain attention, improve understanding and compensate for poor memory – the whole class will benefit (see appendix 10 'Giving and following instructions' on page 66).
- Use pictures and flowcharts to explain rules, routines and narrative sequences (see appendix 6 'Using timelines to support understanding' on pages 59).
- Never underestimate the value of the humble paper and pen! Drawing quickly as you talk on a sketchpad or OHP will instantly raise children's levels of attention and understanding. Don't worry if your drawings are useless – they will be all the more memorable!

Social rules

- Involve class in devising rules for sharing and turn-taking:
  - Demarcate tables with tape, and place hoops or carpet squares on the floor to show personal space, (or explain it as half an arm's length away). Explain rules when crossing into someone else's space, for example, saying excuse me, sorry, please pass the water, shall I do that for you?
  - Use numbers and timers for turn-taking, 'Come in number 6, your time is up'.
  - Get children to put their names on personal items brought to school and explain that when playing with friends' toys these must remain visible and not be put in pockets, bags or trays. If it doesn't have a name on it, it belongs to the school.
  - Trying to stop or ignore interrupting will simply increase it, so explain and practise the three point rule – get my attention, wait for a sign that I am listening, then speak. Agree appropriate ways of getting attention and how to recognise that someone is ready to listen.
  - Encourage children to practise 'good talking' by saying each other's names and waiting for 'Yes' before carrying on with their message or question.

Active listening

- Gain pupils' attention before you speak using clear visual clues to make sure children understand what they have to do (see 'Focus' on page 24).
- Note the pupils who need extra time to process and respond, and give simple repetition initially, rather than rephrasing the question or instruction.
- Rather than testing pupils' recall by immediately asking questions, invite them to share or practise what they have learnt in pairs or small groups.
- Double-check that pupils know what they should be doing by getting them to tell it back in their own words, or by helping them identify keywords to repeat to themselves, write down or draw. For example, 'So *where* are you going? And *who* do you need? And *what* are you asking her? That's it – Class 2 – Sophie – dinner-money'.
- Adopt a whole class policy to develop Active Listening skills so that children are able to seek help or clarification when they do not understand. See appendix 7 'What is an active listener?' on page 63.

Support

- Avoid reinforcing an incorrect or inappropriate answer as this maintains poor comprehension. Accept the information given but reframe it before repeating the original question. For example, 'Oh that's another interesting fact – yes, a chameleon does change colour – that's something it can do so we'll add that here. We were also thinking about what *kind* of animal is it, what other creature does it *look* like?'
- Be explicit and include all steps in any reasoning process – we cannot assume world or social knowledge, even when pupils appear to have an excellent factual knowledge and rote memory.
- Provide teaching assistants with advance lesson plans so they can collect pictures and objects to reinforce vocabulary learning. Use a multi-sensory approach when introducing new vocabulary as this establishes a range of links for subsequent word-recall (see appendix 12 'Introducing new vocabulary' on page 68).
- Avoid dependency on one TA, particularly in secondary school. Better continuity will be achieved if the pupil is supported by two or three individuals who work together in the pupil's best interests.
- As part of an Active Listening policy, ensure that pupils are able to support each other rather than relying solely on adults for clarification and guidance. Ideally the teacher should be the person they leave till last when needing help! See appendix 8 'Giving and seeking clarification' on page 64.
- Sec Display a text message to remind pupils to ask four other people to help before approaching the teacher [C4 ... B4 ... ME].
- Encourage by saying 'This is hard, you're doing so well' rather than 'This is easy, I know you can do it'.

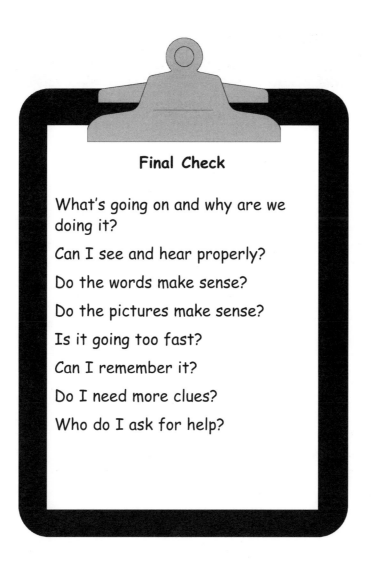

Final Check

What's going on and why are we doing it?

Can I see and hear properly?

Do the words make sense?

Do the pictures make sense?

Is it going too fast?

Can I remember it?

Do I need more clues?

Who do I ask for help?

Useful resources

Writing with Symbols 2000 from Widgit Software Ltd, 124 Cambridge Science Park, Milton Rd, Cambridge CB4 0ZS (Tel: 01223 425 558; www.widgit.com).

Social Skills posters from Taskmaster Ltd, Morris Road, Leicester LE2 6BR (Tel: 0116 270 4286; www.taskmasteronline.co.uk).

Johnson, M. (2005) *Functional Language In the Classroom* (coping strategies for turn-taking and appropriateness). Manchester Metropolitan University Commercial Office, 0161 247 2535.

Johnson, M. & Player, C. (2009) *Active Listening for Active Learning*. Stafford: QEd Publications.

Attention Controls . . . . . SuXess Factor

Signs that tasks are pitched at too high a level to facilitate success include:

- Hesitancy, prefers to copy.
- Over-dependence on adult support, lack of interaction with peers.
- Lack of faith in own judgement.
- Opting out.
- Giving up easily.
- Needs frequent refocusing on task in hand.
- Relates well to animals and younger children (they don't challenge or ask difficult questions).
- Relieved to find distractions.

Factors that maintain motivation and persistence by promoting confidence in ability include:

- Regular experience of task-completion with its intrinsic reward – a sense of achievement and satisfaction.
- Evidence that progress is being made leading to belief that the task is manageable.
- Experience of success or enjoyment with similar tasks.
- Freedom to make mistakes and find own solutions.
- Realistic expectations.

Possible barriers within *school* include:

- Lack of TAs to provide support combined with tendency for TAs to finish tasks for pupils.
- Perceived pressure to focus on targets such as handwriting, scissor skills, communication and phonological awareness before children have pre-requisite skills such as strength, dexterity, eye-hand co-ordination, discrimination, understanding, turn-taking and imaginative play. This can lead to children's first experience of school being associated with effort and confusion rather than fun and achievement.
- Lack of time or knowledge to differentiate the curriculum and break tasks down into smaller steps to ensure success.
- Lack of awareness of natural stages of development leading to unrealistic expectations.
- Lack of training and specialist support to assist teachers in assessing and addressing wide range of need and ability within each class.

Possible barriers within *pupils* include:

- Additional educational needs which are not always identified, acknowledged and catered for.
- Poor organisational skills preventing task-completion, for example, still looking for pencil long after everyone else has finished; unable to methodically approach task.
- Immature attention mechanism – easily distracted so unable to see tasks through.
- Parenting styles which fail to validate or promote child's endeavours and achievements.

How to improve attention and motivation by increasing the SuXess Factor

Task completion

- Ensure that children finish tasks, *ideally at the same time.* This will mean giving some children a head start, for example, when getting changed for P.E., or differentiating tasks so that some children have a shorter task.
- Make class objective to *finish* work rather than to do the *same* work, and to work together as a team in order to meet that objective.
- Give children as much help as they need along the way, but let them *finish* the task themselves so that they have a sense of ownership and achievement.
- Encourage by saying 'This is hard, you're doing so well' rather than 'This is easy, I know you can do it'.
- Ensure that tasks are initially within pupils' capabilities and gradually do one of the following:
  - make the task more complex;
  - make the task longer;
  - reduce the support given.

Realistic targets

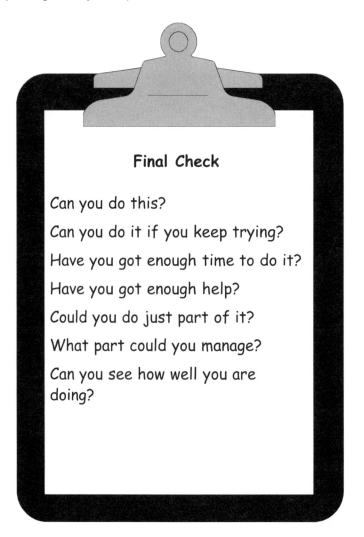

- Bear in mind that trying harder does not make a task easier.
- Differentiate tasks by placing coloured cards/animal pictures etc. on tables. For example, 'If you've got a tiger I want you to go with Jan and tell each other what you did at the weekend; giraffes draw something you did at the weekend and think of a title for it; koalas do a drawing with a title and one or two sentences about what you did.'
- Ensure children are clear about the task objective, what they have to do, how long it will take and how to get help if needed (see Organisation' on page 18).
- Allow reluctant speakers to experience success through non-verbal participation until they are ready to talk (pointing, drawing, puppets, computers etc).
- Become acquainted with normal stages of development (study days, publications, library, internet) to assist in planning appropriate task progression and setting realistic targets (see 'Developmental Progressions' on page 71 for some examples).
- Include all children in at least part of each teaching sequence but modify objectives/activities when concepts are likely to prove too hard for some children. Refer to the Primary National Strategy *Speaking, Listening and Learning: Working with children who have special educational needs* for access strategies, sample lesson plans and a 25 minute video putting theory into practice.

Final Check

Can you do this?

Can you do it if you keep trying?

Have you got enough time to do it?

Have you got enough help?

Could you do just part of it?

What part could you manage?

Can you see how well you are doing?

Useful resources

Johnson, M. & Wintgens, A. (2001) *Selective Mutism Resource Manual.* Speechmark.

Mortimer, H. (2004) *Trackers 0-3.* Stafford: QEd Publications.

Speaking, Listening and Learning: Working with children who have special educational needs, DFES, 1187-2005 G (www.dfes.gov.uk)

Attention Controls . . . . . Motivation

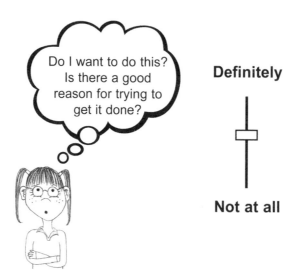

Definitely

Not at all

Signs that underlying difficulties are impacting on motivation include:

- Rejection of task, for example, 'this is boring'.
- Rejection of praise or rewards, for example, 'stickers are stupid'.
- Lack of persistence.
- Requesting alternative activity.
- Looking for distractions.
- Playing the clown.

While presenting as disinterest, such behaviours often indicate that the pupil is overwhelmed by the task (primary school) or believes learning to be a lost cause (secondary school).

Low

Factors that are important for motivation include:

- A sense of purpose.
- Belief that the task is manageable.
- Expectation that any effort involved will lead to a positive outcome (different individuals have different motivators).
- Immediate or deferred gain in one or more of the following areas:
  - enjoyment, excitement, interest;
  - a challenge;
  - personal achievement, satisfaction;
  - learning something new;
  - short or long-term benefit or reward;
  - social approval, acceptance, interaction.
- Mutual respect.

High

Possible barriers within *school* include:

- Significant population of children with unidentified language and learning difficulties.
- Lack of speech and language therapy input and other specialist advice to assist with screening and awareness raising.
- Focus on subject areas and attainment targets rather than individual needs, learning styles and home liaison.
- Lack of resource and manpower.
- Low staff morale.

Possible barriers within *pupils* include:

- History of failure and low self-esteem – see no point in attempting task.
- Purpose of task is not clear due to poor comprehension or inferencing skills.
- Focus is on effort rather than gain (for example, pupil is struggling with handwriting, processing language, eye-hand co-ordination or copying from board and losing the enjoyment of new knowledge and discovery).
- Learned helplessness – inappropriate curriculum differentiation and compensatory teaching strategies perpetuates cycle of failure and opting out.
- Permissive parenting style with lack of boundaries as recognised by 'Why should I?'

How to improve attention by increasing motivation

Purpose

- Recognise that pupils will be driven by different motivators. Typically:
  - low achievers are likely to be people-oriented and can be spurred on by having an important role within a team exercise;
  - pupils with ASD (including Asperger's Syndrome) are likely to be task-oriented and motivated by the need for achievement and closure. They will find it hard to work collectively with other people, and need tasks which enable them to work alone but contribute to a team project.
- Ensure pupils have a clear grasp of the task in hand (see 'Organisation' and 'Understanding' on pages 18 and 33).
- Make the purpose of each task explicit and ensure pupils are aware of the longer term gains (for example, writing invitations as part of planning a Christmas party).
- Ensure pupils know how long a task will last – we are far more accepting of mundane tasks when we know exactly how long they will last and what's coming up next.

Enjoyment

- Build persistence by ensuring that pupils regularly experience task-completion and success (see 'SuXess Factor' on page 38). Pupils need a balance of challenge and achievability.
- A sense of inclusion is important to most learners, and pupils will prefer to miss a *whole* lesson than part of it. If absence is essential, send a runner to collect pupils rather than start a new topic/exercise without them.

- Get to know individual pupils and identify their personal strengths, interests, aspirations and motivators. Ask class to say what each pupil is good at and list each as a positive, for example, 'watching TV' equals 'specialist knowledge'.

- Use pupils' skills and interests in lessons/assignments, and link assignments to their personal visions.
- Be willing to share own shortcomings with humour and positivity.
- Ensure an enthusiastic delivery, building in humour and the element of surprise.
- Avoid 'empty' praise such as 'Great!'; 'Well done!'; 'That's brilliant!' for pupils with low self-esteem (see 'Troubles' on page 45).

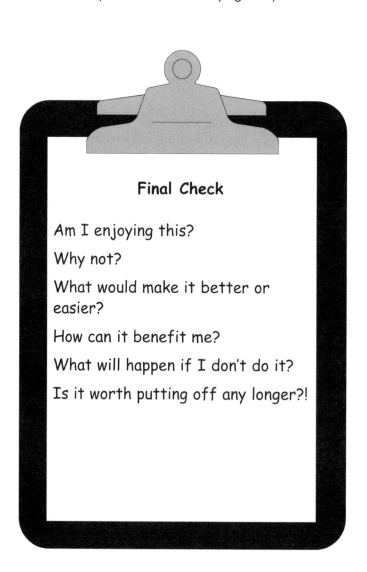

Final Check

Am I enjoying this?

Why not?

What would make it better or easier?

How can it benefit me?

What will happen if I don't do it?

Is it worth putting off any longer?!

Attention Controls . . . . . Troubles

Lots

Nothing

High

Low

Signs that emotional or psychological issues may be affecting concentration and participation include:

- Withdrawn, passive, listless, aggressive, volatile, frozen.
- Avoidance e.g. 'I don't want to', 'It's stupid', 'Do I have to?'
- Reluctance to take risks, go first or make mistakes.
- Reliance on others to initiate contact and conversation.
- Difficulty separating from parent at start of day.
- Resistance to getting ready for school.
- Tummy aches, headaches.
- Looks for adult protection or company.
- Repetitive questioning, not processing answer.
- Gets in with wrong crowd, easily impressed.
- Rejection of praise e.g. 'It's not good, it's useless'.
- Sense of injustice, being hard done by, 'It's not fair'.
- Isolation.
- 'Losing' books and personal possessions.
- Specific fear marked by avoidance e.g. school toilets, dining room.

Factors that are important for a trouble-free sense of well-being include:

- Feeling good about ourselves and our achievements.
- Believing we are valued and liked both for ourselves and for the contribution we make.
- Regular experience of achievement (it is achievement, rather than praise, that builds confidence, persistence and risk-taking).
- Having friends and a sense of group identity.
- Having a sense of routine, security and control over our lives.
- Ability to deal with the unexpected.
- Freedom to make mistakes without disapproval.
- Feeling relaxed and able to contribute in our own time.
- A support structure and the ability to use it.
- Freedom from bullying, discrimination, injustice and anxiety.

Possible barriers within *school* include:

- Inadequate provision and support from outside agencies for pupils with mental health issues.
- Lack of whole-school training to promote identification of hidden learning and communication difficulties and to address the needs of vulnerable pupils with, for example, ASD, Asperger's syndrome, selective mutism.
- Inability to access 'talking therapies' because the pupil is unable to talk when anxious.
- Lack of time/manpower to befriend individual pupils, liaise with parents, develop pastoral care and provide support in the classroom.
- Language and learning difficulties cause children to fatigue easily – but this can be interpreted as laziness and lack of motivation if underlying difficulties go unrecognised.
- Lack of curriculum differentiation or compensatory teaching strategies for pupils with additional educational needs perpetuates cycle of failure, low self-esteem, sense of injustice and disengagement.
- Parents who put onus on school to deal with their child's difficulties.

Possible barriers within *child* include:

- Language difficulties compromise children's ability to request help, express needs, establish relationships and report bullying.
- Social-communication difficulties result in inappropriate behaviour and inability to deal with the unexpected. As a result, pupils with ASD, Asperger's syndrome and ADHD are often rejected by peers and feel isolated and highly anxious. At the same time their naivety makes them vulnerable to bullying, teasing and being led.
- Organisational difficulties leave children feeling overloaded, disoriented and anxious about day-to-day events.
- Children with language and learning difficulties often draw attention to themselves and invite an imbalance of negative feedback from staff and peers. This has an adverse impact on their self-image, especially when reprimanded in front of peers.
- History of failure and negative self-image – pupils cannot trust or accept praise and live up to others' low opinion/expectations.
- When pupils frequently miss the start of lessons due to medical appointments, withdrawal sessions or poor time-keeping, it is difficult to bond with the group and feel included.
- Parenting styles which focus on what the child is doing wrong.
- Lack of routine and consistent role models in the home.
- Attachment disorder – inconsistent or absent parenting in first two years of life leading to lack of trust, insecurity and low self-opinion.
- Specific anxiety disorders, for example, selective mutism, school avoidance phobia, obsessive compulsive disorder (OCD).

How to improve attention by reducing anxiety, unhappiness and frustration

Behaviour

- Try to focus on the *cause* of an unacceptable behaviour rather than the behaviour itself. Show you understand it's tough, and elicit pupil's help in finding solutions. Ask, for example, 'How can we help you be on time?' rather than, 'What must I do to stop you being late?'
- Use this manual to help identify the cause of a behaviour – the answer could be in the sections on Comfort, Focus or Understanding for example. Either there will be some gain for the pupil (e.g. control of anxiety, social contact, reassurance, reduction or removal of a distressing experience) or it will be the result of the interface between environmental factors and the pupil's ability to deal with them. Do not set out to simply eliminate an undesirable behaviour. Aim to remove the cause or replace the behaviour with an acceptable alternative.
- Acknowledge desirable behaviours and achievements, however small. Focus on good points, not bad. Validate by describing actions, for example, 'You've done this poster really neatly and thought of everything, that's going to be an enormous help when the parents arrive'; 'You are colouring really carefully, aren't you?'
- Avoid putting pupil on the defensive or freezing completely when reprimanding or re-stating rules by steering clear of sustained direct eye-contact. Have a chat sitting or walking side by side.
- Be prepared to apologise.

Praise

- Give affirmation and praise publicly and constructive criticism privately. Never belittle pupils and encourage the same respect between peers.
- Give message that you like pupils' company, not just the work they produce. Smile at them! Show an interest in their hobbies/interests, use these where possible in their work.
- Remember that we can only accept praise if we agree with it, so pupils with a poor self-image and low self-esteem may find it meaningless or patronising. Note which pupils cannot accept overt praise (especially in public) and provide reinforcement in a different way. Describe their behaviour and reward through action rather than praise, for example, 'Peter's finished his already – you take first go on the computer Peter'; 'I noticed you showed Dan the right page just now, that was helpful – Dan, how about letting Peter use your pens now?'

Group identity

- Encourage working in pairs rather than in front of whole class. Find the best mix for small groups. Organise group allocation – avoid self-selection which allows vulnerable pupils be left out.
- Ensure pupils have a voice in discussions/decisions and find out the easiest ways for them to make a contribution. Value all forms of communication – showing, pointing, keyboard, email, MSN.

- Pupils prefer to miss a whole lesson than part of it. If absence is necessary, send a runner to collect pupils so they feel included on their return.
- When pupils are late get them involved by asking the rest of the class to recap the lesson for them as soon as is practical. Everyone will benefit. Deal with lateness as a separate issue when others are not present.

Anxiety about routine

- Make liaison with home a priority.
- If children are anxious about separating from parents in the morning and consistency is an issue, provide a photo each day to let the child know who will be picking them up.
- Many naturally anxious children hate transitions rather than actual separation because these spell change and uncertainty. These children need to be fully in control of their anxiety by knowing exactly what is going to happen to them. Give them a fixed routine for when they arrive in the morning. Visual timetables and warnings of any change in routine are essential. Use Timelines (page 59) to improve both their sense of routine and ability to be flexible.
- Ensure continuity in school for anxious children so they only have to contend with one change at a time.
- [Sec] Avoid dependency on one TA, particularly in secondary school. Better continuity will be achieved if the pupil is supported by two or three individuals who work together in the pupil's best interests.
- Note the quiet passive children who lack confidence and need help to take risks. Ensure they are not ignored and have the opportunity to build a non-threatening relationship with both an adult and peer.
- Build confidence to take risks by acknowledging and rewarding what children have already achieved, rather than rewarding what they might achieve. The promise of a gold star for behaviours such as joining in circle time, being first to line up at the door or answering the register, is not going to make the child less anxious about performing these tasks – it simply reinforces failure.
- Extremely anxious children may develop an intense fear (phobia) of social behaviours which most of us take for granted, for example, speaking, eating or using toilets outside the home. In all cases it will be necessary to show the child you understand the fear and to help them face it one tiny step at a time. See appendices 13 and 18 'Facing fears' and 'Small Steps progression for children who talk at home but not at school' on pages 69 and 76.
- If a child is too anxious to speak (selective mutism), ensure that an adult such as a TA befriends and reassures them that there is no need to speak straightaway. Build rapport through non-verbal activities and check that the child is included in class and playground activities. Ensure they are not penalised by their inability to ask for help or access to the toilet. See appendix 18 'Small steps progression for children who talk at home but not at school' on page 76.
- [Sec] Watch for pupils who are not eating/drinking and explore possible reasons with pupil/parents/counsellor as appropriate. Do not assume pupils are dieting – they may be avoiding the secondary effect of needing the toilet. Ensure pupils have a means of being excused, and are not being persecuted when they get there.

Friendship

- Zero-tolerance policy on bullying.
- Do not wait for passive pupils to report bullying, contact them regularly to ask how things are going.
- Active intervention to develop friendship groups/pairings. Social skills groups or lunchtime clubs for developing social awareness, appropriate social behaviour, assertiveness and life-skills.
- Adopt school policies involving buddy systems/circle of friends/peer mediation as appropriate.
- Adequate break and lunchtime supervision with a 'friendship stop' or 'friendship bench' for children to go when they have no-one to play with. Ask for volunteers for the friendship patrol rota and attach high value to the responsibility of being a friend for the week.

Self-esteem

- Ensure tasks are adequately differentiated to ensure understanding and success. Break tasks down to smaller steps, make them shorter or provide more support (see 'SuXess Factor' on page 38).
- Create a culture with a team ethos that recognises that difference is the norm, and that making mistakes is part of learning. Encourage teamwork to ensure everyone is on board and all contributions are valued. Make it safe to say 'I don't know' as it is knowing how to find out the answer that's important. Implement an active listening policy so that children know how to seek help (see 'Understanding' on page 33).
- Do not put children on the spot but allow them to volunteer information non-verbally, contribute ideas later or watch the others if they find it difficult to respond or hate standing out.
- Identify non-challenging, but nonetheless important, roles for children within day-to-day activities so they experience the value and satisfaction in accepting responsibility and doing a job well – for example, two 'helping hands' to take the register, give drinks out and help tidy each week; two pupils to manage the 'Suggestions' box each term.
- Adopt the '3 stars and a wish' approach to providing feedback – identify three positives and one thing that the pupil could focus on (try to improve) next time.
- Use post-it notes rather than red pen when marking.
- [Sec] Ensure that students with anxiety-related communication difficulties are not denied appropriate counselling or Cognitive Behaviour Therapy on the grounds that they don't talk. If talking therapies are indicated to address specific fears or issues of self-image, these can be conducted non-verbally using questionnaires, rating scales, ranking of priorities, goals and anxieties, speech bubbles, writing and drawing.

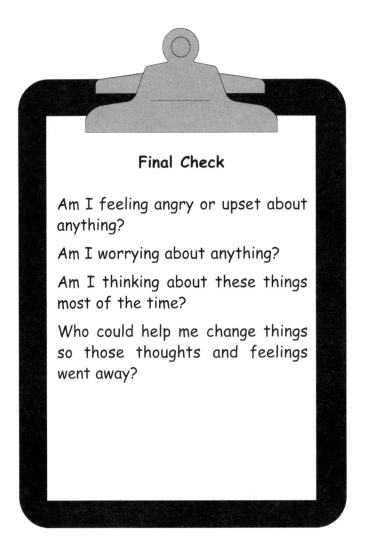

Final Check

Am I feeling angry or upset about anything?

Am I worrying about anything?

Am I thinking about these things most of the time?

Who could help me change things so those thoughts and feelings went away?

Useful resources

Aron, E. (2003) *The Highly Sensitive Child: Helping our children thrive when the world overwhelms them.* London: HarperCollins.

Longo, S. (2006) *My Friend Daniel Doesn't Talk.* Bicester: Speechmark Publications.

Mosley, J. (1998) *More Quality Circle time.* Cambridge: LDA (www.ldalearning.com)

Wheeler, M. (1999) *Toilet Training for Individuals with Autism and Related Disorders: A Comprehensive Guide for Parents and Teachers.* Future Horizons Inc. (UK distributor – Jessica Kingsley Publishers).

Silent Children: Approaches to Selective Mutism. A video/DVD produced by SMIRA and the University of Leicester. Available from smira.leicester@ntlworld.com

Mortimer, H. (2007) *Worry Box: Managing anxiety in young children.* Stafford: QEd Publications.

Mortimer, H. (2007) *Fireworks: Managing anger in young children.* Stafford: QEd Publications.

Useful resources

Aron, E. (2003) *The Highly Sensitive Child: Helping our children thrive when the world overwhelms them.* London: HarperCollins.

DfES (2005) *Speaking, listening, learning: Working with children who have SEN.* Nottingham: DfES Publications (Ref: DfES1187-2005 and DfES1231-2005 to DfES1235-2005). These materials consist of a CDROM, including guidance notes, example adaptations of teaching sequences, a video of an example lesson and accompanying posters.
DfES Publications Centre, PO Box 5050, Annesley, Nottingham, NG15 0DJ
Tel: 0845 60 222 60   Fax: 0845 60 333 60
Email: dfes@prolog.uk.com

Gray, C. (2002) *My Social Stories Book.* London: Jessica Kingsley.

Huebner, D. & Matthews, B. (2005) *What to do when you worry too much: A kid's guide to overcoming anxiety.* Washington DC: Magination Press. You can obtain a catalogue from the Eurospan Group, 3 Henrietta Street, Covent Garden, London WC2E 8LU.

Johnson, M. & Wintgens, A. (2001) *The Selective Mutism Resource Manual.* Bicester: Speechmark Publishing.

Johnson, M. (2005) *Functional Language In the Classroom.* Manchester Metropolitan University.

Johnson, M. & Player, C. (2009) *Active Listening for Active Learning.* Stafford: QEd Publications.

Kidspiration Software, Inspiration Software Inc, 9400 SW Beaverton-Hillsdale Hwy, Suite 300, Beaverton, OR 97005-3300 (www.inspiration.com).

Long, R. (2003) *Understanding Child Behaviour.* London: Quay Books.

Long, R. (2005) *Children's Thoughts and Feelings: Building Success Through Better Behaviour.* London: David Fulton Publishers.

Longo, S. (2006) *My Friend Daniel Doesn't Talk.* Bicester: Speechmark Publishing.

Mortimer, H. (2003) *Trackers 0–3.* Stafford: QEd Publications.

Mortimer, H. (2004) *Trackers 3–5.* Stafford: QEd Publications.

Mortimer, H. (2006) *Music Makers: Music circle times to include everyone.* Stafford: QEd Publications.

Mortimer, H. (2007) *Worry Box: Managing anxiety in young children.* Stafford: QEd Publications.

Mortimer, H. (2007) *Fireworks: Managing anger in young children.* Stafford: QEd Publications.

Mosley, J. (1998) *More Quality Circle time.* Cambridge: LDA (www.ldalearning.com).

Oussoren Voors, R. (2000) *Write Dance: A Progressive Music and Movement Programme for the Development of Pre-writing and Writing Skills in Children.* Bristol: Lucky Duck Publishers.

Passy J. (1993) *Cued Articulation*. Ponteland: STASS Publications.

Silent Children: Approaches to Selective Mutism. A video/DVD produced by SMIRA and the University of Leicester. Available from smira.leicester@ntlworld.com

Smith, C. (2003) *Writing and Developing Social Stories: Practical Interventions in Autism*. Bicester: Speechmark Publishing.

Wheeler, M. (1999) *Toilet Training for Individuals with Autism and Related Disorders: A Comprehensive Guide for Parents and Teachers*. Future Horizons Inc. (UK distributor – Jessica Kingsley Publishers).

● ●

Suppliers

Brain Gym
Educational Kinesiology UK Foundation, 12 Golders Rise, London NW4 2HR
Tel: 020 8202 3141; www.braingym.org.uk

Chewy Tubes
Kapitex Healthcare Ltd, Kapitex House, 1 Sandbeck Way, Wetherby,
West Yorkshire LS22 7GH
Tel: 01937 580211

Makaton Symbols
Makaton Vocabulary Development Project, 31 Firwood Drive, Camberley, Surrey GU15 3QD
Tel: 01276 61390; mvdp@makaton.org; www.makaton.org

Mov'n'Sit Cushion
Epsan Waterfly (UK) Ltd
Tel: 01299 829213; salesuk@waterfly.com; www.epsanwaterfly.com

JPM Products Ltd
Units 11-12 Crane Mead Business Park, Crane Mead, Ware, Hertfordshire SG12 9PZ
Tel: 01920 468 380; sales@jpmproducts.co.uk; www.jpmproducts.co.uk

Social Skills posters and Time Timer
Taskmaster Ltd, Morris Road, Leicester LE2 6BR
Tel: 0116 270 4286; info@taskmasteronline.co.uk; www.taskmasteronline.co.uk

Widgit Rebus Symbols
Widgit Software Ltd
Tel: 01223 425558; info@widgit.com; www.widgit.com/widgitrebus

Appendices

Support Materials

Developmental Progressions

Dry Wipes

[Linear alternatives to Mindmap layout]

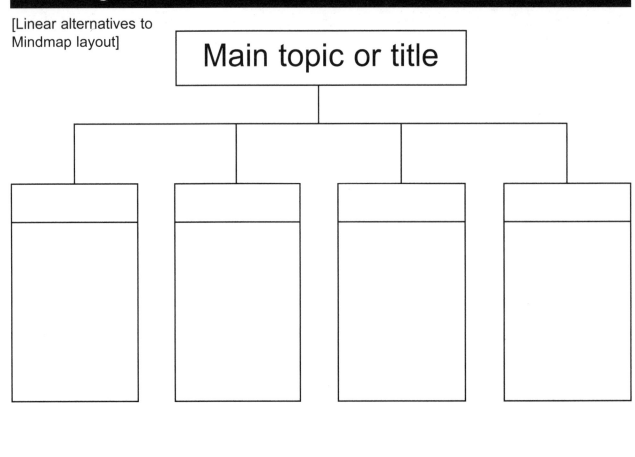

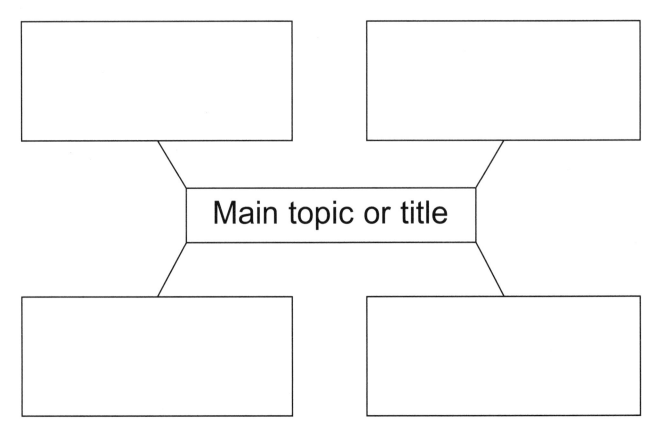

Work plan 1
(add words, pictures or symbols

TASK	How long?

↓

What do I need? (make a list)

↓

What do I have to do?

1. Get everything I need
2.

↓

What to do when finished

1. Read all through your task.
    ASK IF YOU DO NOT UNDERSTAND

    > Prepare!
    > Plan!
    > Do!
    > Check!

2. Think what to do first, then what to do next.

3. Write it down if you need to.

    1.

    2.

    3.

    4.

    5.

    6.
    ↓   until you have finished.

4. Make a list of all the things you need to complete the task.

5. Put away everything that you do **NOT** need and make sure you have enough space to work in.

6. Get all the things you need.

7. **DO IT!**

8. If it is written down, cross off each stage as you do it.

9. Check you have done what was asked.

10. Tell an adult you have finished.

Lesson plan

Date _____

Today we are learning _____

_____

because_____

_____

and the teacher is looking for_____

_____

_____

Today we learnt_____

_____

_____

Next time we will try to/we will _____

_____

_____

Classroom support form

Class: **Subject:**   **Term:**

Learning outcomes for: _____ (Name)

Topic: _____

Expectations	Outcomes	
From the lessons covering this topic, the pupil will be able to:	Pupil's achievements* and comments	Date
perform the following SKILLS:		
demonstrate the following ATTITUDES: • feel good about self • enjoy learning		
understand the following CONCEPTS:		
know the following FACTS:		
Other:		

Key*:   [1] Achieved independently   [2] Achieved with peer support
         [3] Achieved with intermittent adult support   [4] Achieved with 1:1

Signed: _____   _____
            Teaching assistant   **Class teacher/SENCO**

Do you find yourself saying the same thing over and over again but it never sinks in? In many situations children are not able to process language, but can understand through visuals – *Timelines* could be your answer!

The 'Here and Now' child

Timelines are an extremely simple way to help 'here and now' children deal with abstract concepts, inference and social understanding. These children cope much better with the language of concrete experience – language as it relates to objects, pictures and actions that are right in front of them. They are quick with the running commentary, prefer practical demonstration to explanation and are captured by visual images rather than verbal explanations.

Just like books, films and a well-developed imagination, Timelines bring the 'there and then' into a child's visual experience so they can begin to relate to events in other locations and timeframes, and understand the reasoning inherent in warnings, assurances, consistencies and changes in routine. Using a sequence of simple pictures, symbols or words, Timelines provide a visual reference to hold the child's interest and illustrate the spoken word. Prepared in advance or produced as you talk, as an accompaniment to Social Stories or as a stand-alone, Timelines can be used with children from 3 years of age into adulthood to achieve an immediate improvement in understanding.

Routines and narrative

Add simple pictures, symbols or words to the boxes to represent a sequence of activities or events, with clear pathways to illustrate alternative endings, choices and changes in routine. Timelines help children become less confused, more flexible and more secure, and promote the development of prediction and imagination in story-telling.

Social understanding, rules and behavioural expectations

Add simple pictures, symbols or words to the boxes to show options, conditions and acceptable behaviour. It will also be possible to let children 'see into the future' by showing what will happen as a consequence of inappropriate behaviour. These could be social consequences such as having no-one to play with, or sanctions such as no time left to go on the computer. By contrasting these consequences with positive outcomes and rewards, Timelines provide children with a true choice and are far more effective than verbal explanation, disapproval or admonishment.

Imagination and reasoning

Once familiar with the construct of Timelines, children can be involved in completing, manipulating and producing their own in activities such as planning a birthday party, devising rules, précising a story and writing a new ending. Remember that timelines are about a flow of ideas and thinking 'in the right direction', so in the initial stages speed, not accuracy, is of the essence. You do not have to be a good artist to produce an effective Timeline!

Timelines: Standard formats

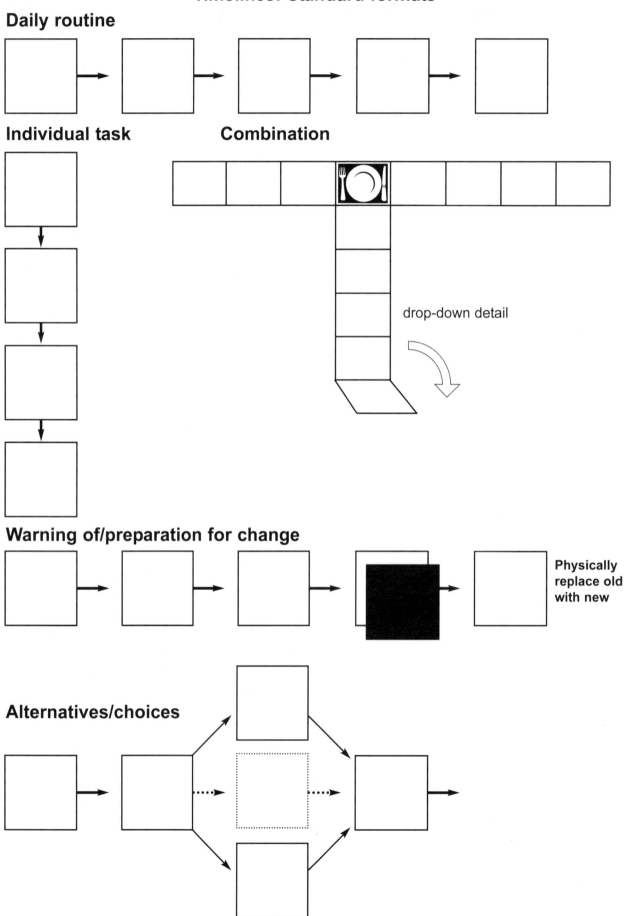

Daily routine

Individual task

Combination

drop-down detail

Warning of/preparation for change

Physically replace old with new

Alternatives/choices

Simultaneous action ('while . . .')

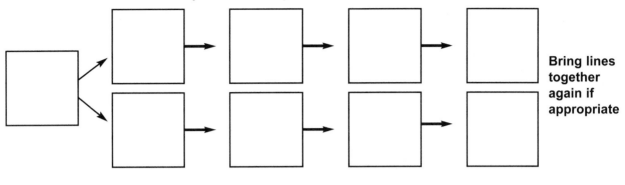

Bring lines together again if appropriate

Identifying consequences of choice/behaviour ('it depends . . .')

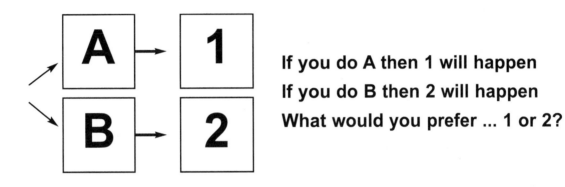

If you do A then 1 will happen

If you do B then 2 will happen

What would you prefer ... 1 or 2?

Anticipating outcomes ('it depends . . .')

First use diagram as above: If A applies, 1 follows; if B applies then 2 follows (can include more variables C3, D4 as required).

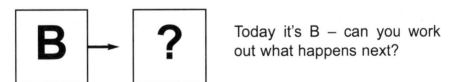

Today it's B – can you work out what happens next?

Surprises

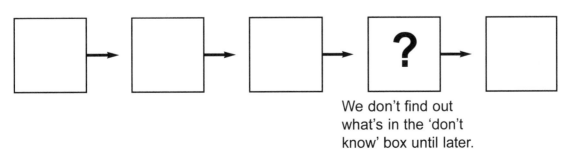

We don't find out what's in the 'don't know' box until later.

Examples of timelines

Consequences of behaviour . . .

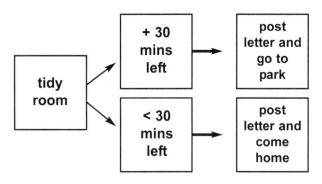

Choices . . .

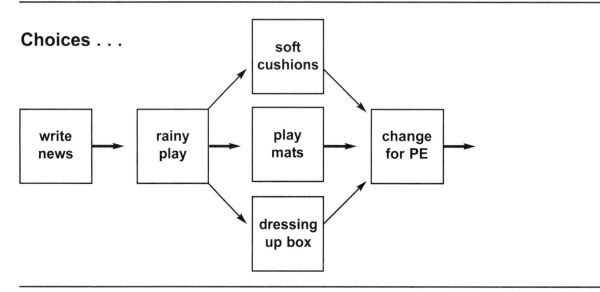

Surprises . . .

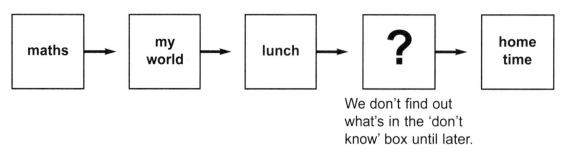

We don't find out what's in the 'don't know' box until later.

It depends . . .

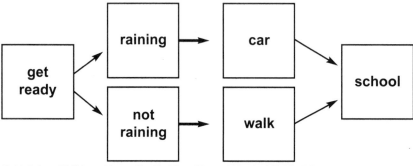

What is an active listener? Appendix 7

Someone who realises that messages cannot always be understood, and takes responsibility for seeking clarification when confused, stuck or unsure.

Whole class strategies for developing active listening skills

1) Develop class rules for 'good listening':
   - sit quietly in your own space **'good sitting'**
   - look at or face the speaker **'good looking'**
   - think about the words **'good thinking'**
   - wait – one person at a time **'good waiting'**

2) Create a 'safe' environment – give children permission to question, challenge and admit uncertainty – as long as they do it politely!

3) Respond positively to requests for information, and the ability to say 'I don't know' or 'I don't understand'.

4) Promote the idea that it's 'good to ask'. Flag up the benefits of seeking help or clarification using good role models – children need to see that everybody asks questions and gets stuck from time to time.

5) Indicate your own need for clarification, rather than guessing.

6) Avoid giving children more information as soon as they get stuck, as this removes both the need and opportunity for them to practise seeking help independently. Suggest appropriate clarification strategies instead. For example, 'It's difficult to hear me with everyone talking, isn't it? If you need me to say any of these again, just say "A bit louder please". Shall I say that one again a bit louder?'

7) Give children practice in deciding if requests or instructions make sense, and seeking clarification when they don't (e.g. during circle time).

8) Encourage children to check with each other before going to an adult.

9) Adopt consistent language and class rules for guessing:
   - 'guessing' = giving an answer when you don't know if it's right (it might be wrong! So first check it's OK to guess);
   - 'having a go' = trying to answer when people know you're not sure;
   - 'working it out' = using clues to get the right answer.

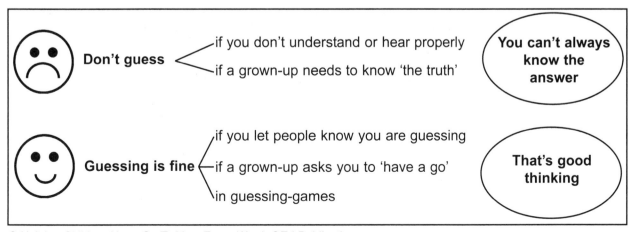

Giving and seeking clarification

Appendix 8

Suggestions for classroom discussion/policy

No-one understands everything – I can't always understand you, and you don't always understand me. How do we feel when that happens?

It's much nicer to feel like this!

We know this will happen, so let's agree on what we can do when . . .

A. You try to tell me something but I don't understand

1) I will let you know I don't understand.

2) You need to do one or more of the following:
   - say it again trying to put in all the sounds;
   - explain it a different way or give me a clue;
   - mime it;
   - draw it;
   - point to it or show me;
   - leave it – people often take a while to work things out. We can always try again later.

B. I am talking to you but you don't understand

1) You need to let me know you don't understand.

2) Do you need me to:
   - say all or part of it again?
   - explain it a different way?
   - tell you what one or more of the words mean?
   - show you or draw it?
   - write it down?
   - give you a clue (more information)?

C. I ask the class to do something but you're not sure what to do

1) See if the person next to you can explain (*they must not do it for you*).

2) If neither of you know what to do, check with the rest of the table.

3) If none of you know, put your hands up or ask _____ to come over.

4) If _____ doesn't know, one of you needs to ask the teacher/put your Help! sign up/post a Q in the question box (select as appropriate).

Less talk, more action!

Strategies to engage visual and kinaesthetic learners in the classroom

Aim: to make curriculum activities more accessible and enjoyable by reducing emphasis on language processing and literacy.

1. Pupils with language and learning difficulties will lose attention and become quickly demotivated if there is a heavy emphasis on listening, reading and writing on top of taking on board new information. Ideally, language and literacy learning will take place as standalone activities and consolidated, rather than extended, in other subject areas.

    - Provide photocopied notes or worksheets rather than asking pupils to copy from the board.
    - Reduce text on worksheets by substituting pictures for text, or use symbols software* to add a picture or symbol above each word.
    - Reduce need to write by allowing pupils to complete worksheets by cutting and pasting answers in place, or circling the correct word or phrase.

2. Get pupils moving as much as possible.

    - Demonstrate concepts by using pupils to represent points on a map, parts of a machine, events on a timeline etc.
    - Use actions to aid memory (e.g. create a story or sequence of hand movements to link a list of people, places, objects or events).
    - Use models and then pupils themselves to act-out and develop narrative themes, historical events, social dilemmas etc.
    - Encourage pupils to walk around as they read or revise.
    - List key facts on index cards for pupils to shuffle, categorise and flick through.

3. Support spoken word with visuals to increase attention and understanding.

    - Draw as you talk, aiming for speed not accuracy.
    - Clarify instructions through demonstration and/or flowcharts.
    - Get pupils to repeat demonstration/explanation in small groups or to whole class.
    - Make deliberate mistakes for pupils to spot and correct.
    - Use interactive whiteboard to demonstrate concepts such as size and position.
    - Communicate through puppets, masks, gesture, signs and symbols.
    - Maintain eye-contact, lip-reading and facial expression with pupils by using an OHP or standing at side of interactive whiteboard.

4. Engage pupils through music, rhythm and sounds.

    - Repeat key points or lists using raps and rhythms.
    - Use background music to help set scene, explore characters, create a calm environment.

* e.g. Symbols 2000 software from Widgit Software Ltd, 124 Cambridge Science Park, Milton Rd, Cambridge CB4 0ZS (Tel: 01223 425558; www.widgit.com/widgitrebus).

Giving and following instructions Appendix 10

Whole class strategies to improve understanding

1) Talk as you would to a group of foreign language pupils, assuming there are going to be comprehension difficulties. Use language you are comfortable with, relying on *pauses* and *visuals* to get your message across.

2) Don't speak slower but pause more often. Highlight new vocabulary and teaching points by pausing before and after key words and phrases.

3) Warn pupils when several instructions are coming up, tell them how many and itemise each step with a keyword plus simple drawing or symbol. Get class to recap key words or place instructions in correct order before starting activity.

4) Tell pupils no-one understands everything so they are bound to have difficulty at times. Ensure they know how to obtain help (see appendix 8 'Giving and seeking clarification' on page 64 and appendix 7 'What is an active listener?' on page 63).

5) Passive pupils may benefit from a Help! sign to put on their table.

6) Clarify instructions through demonstration, and encourage pupils to use talk and mime to memorise sequences before carrying them out.

7) Demonstrate tasks, making deliberate mistakes for pupils to spot and correct. Discuss what will happen if steps are carried out in the wrong order, acting this out with humour where possible (providing this does not encourage pupils to laugh at each other's mistakes).

8) Invite pupils who understand to start. Then repeat the demonstration or instructions and keywords for the remainder of the group.

9) Get pupils who understand at one table to go over to another table to explain. Later ask the second table what they've just been told.

10) Get class to explain to late-comers what the lesson has been about and what they are about to do.

11) Support verbal explanation with demonstration or simple diagrams, symbols, drawings and checklists set out in clearly demarcated rows and columns. Minimise overload by providing previously prepared worksheets, handouts and writing-frames.

12) Differentiate tasks by colour/animal etc., for example, '*reds* draw something you did at the weekend and think of a title for it, *greens* do a drawing with a title and one sentence about what you did, *blues* do a drawing with a title and two paragraphs'. The goal is to *finish* rather than be the same.

13) Ask for volunteers or assign buddies to support peers.

14) Explain how pupils can *help* each other but not *do* each other's work i.e.

   ✔ **tell** what equipment is needed, what to do and what to put away

   ✔ **show** where things are, where to start and what to change

   ✘ **do** the work or **give** the answer.

N.B. When we ask pupils to help us, we usually want them to *do* something for us, so it's not surprising they get confused!

Analysing children's responses to questions Appendix 11

Child's name: _____ Class: _____

Completed by: _____ Date: _____

Sample questions and answers
1.
2.
3.
4.
5.

Language Area		1	2	3	4	5
Not aware of being addressed (A, SC, H)						
Doesn't realise a response is required (SC)						
Says nothing, appears anxious or at a loss (E, U)						
Frozen expression (E)						
Echoes all or part of question	Doesn't seem to understand purpose of Q (SC)					
	Seems to need more time to think (U)					
Off target (answers a different question) (U, SC, H) (e.g. What's *happening* in this picture? It's a jungle).						
Gives an associated or made-up word (word-finding difficulty) (e.g. **toadstool** = frog-chair/**toa**ster.						
Hears a key-word and gives an associated response (U, SC, H) (e.g. What colour is the **sky**? Martian invaders came in flying saucers).						
Literal interpretation (U, SC)						
Gives more information than is needed (SC, U)						
Answers show lack of common-sense/unusual logic (SC)						
Incomplete answer	Lacking in information (U, SR, E)					
	Lacking in grammatical words/rules (SR)					
Responds to only part of Q/can't answer Qs about story (U, M, H)						
Can't cope with open-ended Qs/choice/subjective info (SC, E)						
Delayed development (U, G)	Not understanding basic what/who/where Qs					
	Not coping with Qs about objects/people if out-of-sight					
	Confuses where/when					
	Not understanding basic how/why					
	Can't cope with Qs about past/future events					
	Can't cope with Qs involving reasoning e.g. odd-man-out, classification, inference, alternatives					
Seems to know answer but response can't be understood (Sp)						
Doesn't ask for repetition/clarification	Lacks coping strategies and active listening skills					
Opts out, changes subject, creates diversion						

SC = social communication   **A** = attention & listening   **U** = understanding/vocabulary   **H** = hearing   **E** = emotional
SR = sentence structure/grammatical rules   **M** = memory   **Sp** = speech sounds   **G** = general factors/delay

Introducing new vocabulary

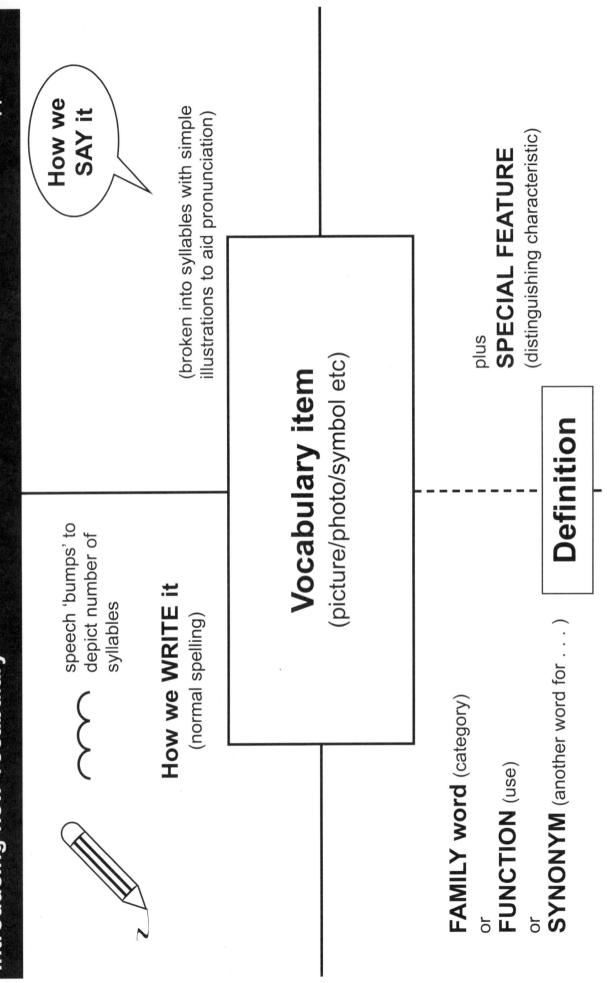

How we SAY it

(broken into syllables with simple illustrations to aid pronunciation)

speech 'bumps' to depict number of syllables

How we WRITE it (normal spelling)

Vocabulary item
(picture/photo/symbol etc)

plus **SPECIAL FEATURE** (distinguishing characteristic)

Definition

FAMILY word (category)

or

FUNCTION (use)

or

SYNONYM (another word for . . .)

Supporting the anxious and phobic child at school

Most children experience fears at some stage – fear of the dark, strangers, dogs or images on the TV screen for example. Some may struggle with their fears in make-believe play or nightmares, seeing or acting out scenes of imprisonment, death and violence. Others may find a sympathetic ear to acknowledge the reality of their fears and help put those fears in perspective.

With reassurance that the role-models in the child's life also had fears when they were younger, and support to gradually confront fears (e.g. choosing a night light together and shutting the door a little more each night) most children come to school equipped to face the world and its challenges. For those born with an anxious personality however, fears may have developed which have little to do with the focus of fear itself. Such fears, or phobias, will be marked by intense avoidance (appearing as refusal) and sudden changes in the child's general demeanour when they experience panic.

How phobias arise

Phobias develop when experiencing intense anxiety for reasons unknown to the child at the same time as exposure to a specific situation which the child can readily identify. For example, a fear of talking to non-family members may result from being left alone and associating the separation anxiety with the determined efforts of a stranger to elicit conversation.

It can be very difficult for schools to deal with apparently irrational fears such as speaking, eating, getting changed or using toilets outside the home. In all cases it will be necessary to show the child you understand the fear and to help them face it one tiny step at a time. However:

- Do not dismiss the fear as nothing to worry about.
- Do not ignore the situation and try to take the child's mind off the fear.

These messages imply that the child is being silly or weak, and that the fear is too powerful to face. The fear remains to fester or return in various forms. Better to acknowledge that it is natural to feel afraid and reassure that things get less frightening as we learn about them and have friends and family to help us gradually overcome them.

One tiny step at a time

A good rule of thumb is to start with situations the child can manage and to gradually change one thing at a time. This may involve bringing parents in to assist with the transition between home and school, or breaking an anxiety down into several components which can be tackled separately. For example:

- Overcoming a fear of using the school toilets might start with getting used to the noise of the hand-dryer;
- A reluctance to get changed for PE might be removed by assuring the child they will not be singled out to demonstrate activities unless they put their hand up to volunteer.

A programme of small-steps targets can be a very effective way of helping children face their fears and become increasingly confident in trying new things. For example, Jack was 'refusing' to eat at dinner time as he was overwhelmed by the noise and jostling in the dining room. Targets included:

- eating with a trusted adult in a separate room to his peers;
- going into the dining hall with the adult ahead of the other children and eating with his best friend;
- going into the dining room with his best friend ahead of the other children.

Avoidance or refusal?

Anxious children are often described as stubborn and controlling. Remember that the child is desperately trying to avoid an anxiety attack and that their reluctance to comply is the only coping strategy they know. These children can only face and dispel their fears by knowing exactly what is going to happen next and trusting that things will move at their pace. We need to give them more control, not less!

Age	Attention Level*	Postural Support (needed in order to attend to external objects or activities)	Group Participation
0–1	Fleeting attention, easily distracted.	Total support (e.g. beanbag, cushions, adult's lap).	Operating as an individual. Showing interest in other children. Only responds to adults when they enter personal space (30-40cm from child).
1–2	Attends to own choice of activity. Momentarily distracted by adult's choice of activity.	Only tolerates confinement at mealtimes. Standing, moving between activity stations, climbing steps and solid furniture.	Copies leader and rest of group with 1:1 adult support. Beginning to listen with group for a cue before performing action.
2–3	Can switch attention to adult's choice of activity with firm direction. Can only concentrate on one thing at a time, involving either looking, listening or doing.	Needs body support to stay still (e.g. kneeling or lying on floor, sitting in buggy, armchair or on sofa).	Increases sitting and waiting time for shared activities such as story and snack time. Beginning to take turns and repeat same activity in a small circle.
3–4	Can switch and sustain attention more easily but still focuses on only one thing at a time, i.e. needs to stop activity in order to listen.	Low chairs, preferably with arms, with feet on floor or footrest. Sitting on floor leaning against wall or furniture.	Listening and turn-taking in a small circle. Different roles within group activity if adult-managed.
4–5	Beginning to integrate focus of attention for short spells (e.g. can listen to speaker while continuing task).	Low chairs without arms, sometimes at table, feet on floor. Sitting on floor with crossed feet, resting elbows on legs.	Listening and turn-taking in a large circle. Group discussion. Negotiates different roles in playground without adult support.
5–6	Can successfully integrate focus of attention and sustain for longer periods (e.g. can talk to neighbour while completing task and notice when teacher gives new instruction).	Sitting at tables, feet on floor, and elbows supported. Benches do not offer adequate support for more than a few minutes.	Listening and turn-taking in a large circle. Group discussion. Negotiates different roles in playground without adult support.

*Developmental stages of attention Cooper, J., Moodley, M. & Reynell, J. (1978)

Natural development of play

Stage	Physical (dexterity and co-ordination)	Pretend (thinking and imagination)	Verbal (language development and communication)	Social (interest in others and appreciation of their needs)
Awareness of immediate environment	Attention drawn to rattles, shakers, mobiles – no control yet to reach, grip, release objects.	Responds only to immediate needs and items in vision.	Enjoys soothing sounds and watching faces; Imitates facial expression.	Develops trust and security through consistent, positive handling; Sensitive to others' emotions.
Awareness of self	Explores environment; Toys in mouth; Throws objects (especially if they come back!); Bangs/joins objects together.	Notes how objects are used and repeats this in play (e.g. feeds doll, pushes car along, stirs spoon in cup).	Sound-play (babble); Imitates gestures and sounds; Starts to imitate words and then develop words of their own.	Develops sense of self as distinct from others; Repetitive turn-taking games with simple sounds/action – anticipates and 'asks' for more.
Discovering how the world works	Looks for hidden objects; Cause-effect play – tries things out over and over; Relates objects to each other, exploring in/on/up/down relationships; Early matching and sorting; Sand and water play.	Makes puppet/toy perform actions; Pretends object is something else (e.g. lolly-stick becomes a spoon); Uses absent objects in play (e.g. serves out imaginary cake, pretends to fill kettle).	Makes animal/car sounds etc.; Wants same book over and over and names pictures; Joins in action songs and rhymes with adult; Provides running commentary and links several actions together (e.g. feeds doll and puts to bed).	Solitary play – plays alongside rather than with other children; Initiates play with adults (e.g. blowing bubbles); Can eventually follow adult's change of direction.
Imaginary – logical	Creative play – painting, cooking, making, sticking; Active play – tricycle, play apparatus, rough and tumble; Jigsaws.	Make-believe play (e.g. dressing-up, shops); Acts out recent events and stories using toys.	Learns action rhymes and songs and knows what comes next; Guessing games involving mime and descriptions; Makes dolls/toys talk to each other while acting out a story.	Joins in singing and movement activities in small groups; Needs an adult or older child's help to sustain interaction with peers and take turns.
Imaginary – creative	Construction toys involving greater dexterity.	Extended house play and dramatic make-believe (monsters etc.).	Talks to other children during play and waits for answer; Enjoys sound-play: making silly words and generating rhymes; Invents stories.	Co-operative play with peers – beginning to set rules without an adult; 6+ Negotiative play – less self-centred.

72

© Helping Children Hang On To Your Every Word, QEd Publications

The development of pretend play

Pretend play develops in two distinct but overlapping phases as described below. Most children have passed through these stages of development by the time they go to school, but some will need structured support beyond their pre-school years to help them play creatively and imaginatively with children their own age.

Imaginative play shows that a child is ready to use language to predict, plan and problem-solve. By supporting a child's play development, we are therefore supporting the development of flexible, creative thought and language.

We can help by being aware of how children currently play and joining in at their level. When they are enjoying shared rather than solitary play, we can introduce activities from the next stage. At first we will need to demonstrate these activities and encourage the child to join in or copy. Gradually we can suggest (rather than show) what the child could do with the toys or objects. Eventually the child may be able to contribute their own ideas.

Golden rules   Show pleasure in all the child does (within reason!).
Join in whenever possible.
Extend the play sequence with one more idea if you have the child's attention.

Phase 1: Functional (Representative) play

Children use objects (including miniature representations of real objects) in ways appropriate to their conventional function. They gradually extend play to include statements/actions such as 'It's hot!'

Functional play is characterised by stereotyped, predictable sequences/language.
*   simple functional play with large objects, e.g. feed doll;
*   simple role, or situational make-believe play, e.g. act out a recent event or make puppet/toy perform familiar actions;
*   meaningful play sequences, e.g. dolls tea-party.

Phase 2: Symbolic (Imaginative) play

Substitution	Children use an object as if it were another object or person, e.g. stick becomes a snake; matchbox = bed; banana = telephone; bricks used to make a bridge or road.
Attribution	Children attribute properties to an object/person which it does not have, e.g. pretend to be an elephant; pretend cup has broken; doll = good or bad; doll becomes 'Mummy'.
Reference to absent object	Children refer to absent object/person as if they were present, e.g. bite imaginary apple; play with imaginary friend; pretend fire-engine is coming.

*   use of miniature toys to act out different characters in a scenario;
*   make-believe play involving invented people/objects;
*   extended and dramatic make-believe and dressing-up games, e.g. playhouse, shops, doctors and nurses;
*   creative craftwork, e.g. making a snake out of cotton reels;
*   guessing games involving mime, e.g. 'Who Am I?

Anticipation

Early turn-taking games teach the baby to anticipate what comes next and wait for it. Anticipation develops from repeated use of action-based verbal routines (sequences). Picture books build on this at a visual/verbal level – child anticipates what is coming up over the page and begins to answer questions about illustrations: 'What does the cow say?'; 'Where's Spot hiding?' etc.

Targets – for child to enjoy and join in repetitive activity;
      – to be able to predict next action/part of story;
      – to answer simple questions appropriately.

Daily routine and internal timeline

Child identifies, learns and adapts simple sequences in day-to-day life, bath-time, getting ready for school, changing for PE etc. By recognising recurring patterns and boundaries between routines, child can assess time of day – what they have done already and what is coming up later. They can place themselves on a timeline relating to today, past and future.

Targets – for child to relate to picture sequences of daily routines, to predict next picture, insert missing picture and arrange pictures in correct order;
      – to know basic daily routine off by heart;
      – to understand concepts 'first', 'next', 'last' in relation to L ➤ R sequence;
      – to understand concepts 'after', 'before' in relation to L ➤ R sequence.

      N.B. Later, child will extend internal timeline to include awareness of 'tomorrow', 'yesterday', days of the week, seasons, months and years.

Telling news

This starts with prompting and helping child to 'Tell Daddy what we've just been doing' etc. Child will not be able to recall or record their news until they have had practice talking, drawing and writing about what they are doing, as they do it. From the age of about 3 to 5 we can introduce a structure of closed questions.

Targets – for child to use When/Who/Where (and later Why?) structure to recall and record their news (When? component is usually supplied, e.g. 'at the weekend');
      – to recognise what other children have omitted and ask for information.

Simple story sequences

Play is the basis of all story telling and writing as children use it as a vehicle to develop their imaginations. Children learn that real objects, events and attributes can be represented symbolically – by miniatures/models, object-substitutes (a box becomes a car etc.); mime and words – the most abstract substitute of all (e.g. 'ouch, it's hot!' while eating imaginary porridge).

Early repetitive play sequences provide the basis for extending, adapting and inventing new sequences.

A parallel developing interest in books both consolidates and inspires these early play sequences in pictorial form with accompanying language.

Targets   – for child to participate in pretend play using object substitution and mime;
         – to know what will happen next using cause-effect picture cards;
         – to describe a simple picture story sequence recognising links between pictures (*no inference required*);
         – to use simple conjunctions;
         – to discuss/provide alternative endings;
         – to add more detail to story than is shown in pictures alone.

Extended story sequences

Through the use of mime, drama and developing world-knowledge and social awareness, children learn to infer beyond the immediate here and now of a simple picture and to attribute emotions and intent to story characters.

Targets   – to plug gap between two pictures (e.g. cat by goldfish bowl; bowl smashed);
         – to interpret and describe picture story sequences requiring inference;
         – to use more advanced conjunctions;
         – to discuss/provide reasons for behaviour of characters and express opinion regarding appropriateness/acceptability of behaviour;
         – to discuss a possible story behind a single picture (e.g. what the characters are like, what is likely to happen next and what has lead up to the event).

Creative writing

From recording their news, drawing pictures of favourite characters, making books about themselves, and enjoying and re-enacting familiar stories, children develop the ability to relate and record their own stories supported by the structure of beginning/middle/end and closed questions.

Targets   – to use a story plan to brainstorm ideas for a story in a group;
         – to use a story plan to identify key points and record a story in pictures or words based on recall of own experience or familiar story;
         – to use a story plan for creative writing, fading out visual/verbal prompt.

Small steps progression for children who talk at home but not at school

Stage	Characterised by	Goals
1	**No communication** nor participation	For the child to: • watch as key person demonstrates game or activity; • feel unpressured and look forward to sessions with key person.
2	**Cooperation** but no communication	• participate in key person's choice of activity and co-operate with requests/ suggestions pertaining to the execution of that activity.
3	Communication through **visual, non-vocal** means	• use gesture to communicate (nodding, pointing, signing); • take turns with the key person; • give and receive items on request.
4	Use of **non-verbal sound** with key person in a specific setting	• make audible sounds using musical instruments and body parts; • make vocal sounds in key person's presence (laughter, kazoo, environmental noises or letter sounds).
5	Speech **within earshot** of key person	• speak when alone or with immediate family, and allow key person to enter room while still speaking*.
6	Use of **single words** with key person	• produce single words at normal volume* and with appropriate eye-contact in structured situation.
7	**Connected speech** with key person	• produce sentences at normal volume* and with appropriate eye-contact in structured situation.
8**	Connected speech with a **range of people**	• initiate verbal communication with key person; • speak with a selected group of people without key person present (add one person at a time).
9**	Connected speech in a **range of settings**	• speak to selected people in a variety of familiar surroundings without key person present; • speak in unplanned situations.
10	**Free communication**	• speak in any setting *within earshot of others* (e.g. contribute spontaneously to classroom discussion); • speak to strangers.

Programme: **two or three 10-15 minute sessions with the child per week, letting child know exactly what they are going to do in each session. Reward with a sticker at the end of the session for stages 1-4, and more often as child gets closer to communication.**

* A very quiet voice is perfectly acceptable initially and will increase in volume as child gains confidence. Whispering should never be set as a target however, nor accepted when target is a quiet voice, as it can become a difficult habit to break.

** Stages 8 and 9 are covered in tandem, making just one change at a time.

A vital concept in reading readiness is awareness that a WHOLE unit of sound is made of several PARTS. Through typical speech development, babble and experimentation, children learn in sequence that:

- **phrases** are made of single **words**;
- **words** are made of stressed and unstressed **syllables**;
- **syllables** are made of a sequence of **sounds** (phonological awareness).

Children learn through having a go and making mistakes! They copy segments of speech and put them together in a trial and error fashion until they can produce more adult-sounding sentences. Alphabetic knowledge and spelling rules come much, much later. Not all children pass through these stages naturally so literacy programmes need to include:

- an emphasis on **vocabulary** and **phonological awareness**;
- blending practice (**synthesis**) to support the development of **segmentation** skills.

N.B. Progress will be fast-tracked by using *visual* frameworks to support poor listening skills.

Developing awareness of word-boundaries

1) Give instructions as single words without expression, with pauses between each word (for example: Give . . . . the . . . . rabbit . . . . some . . . . carrot). Can children work out what you mean? Add natural intonation if anyone needs a clue. Young children will enjoy this if they are asked to translate 'Robot Talk' into normal speech.

2) Write a phrase or sentence on a strip of paper, illustrating the main words with a simple picture or symbol above the word. Cut up and place individual words face down in the right order, separated by gaps. Say words one at a time, as you point to each piece of paper. When children demonstrate understanding by copying with a fluent phrase or sentence, or by pointing to a matching picture, they turn the words over to make a connected sentence.

3) Reverse the above activity by saying a short phrase (join two or more words together without pausing) as you run your finger across the correct number of face down cards. Can children separate the words in their mind and identify the word on each card? Make it easier by asking for just the last word (they complete the phrase). Be sure to include words of more than one syllable (e.g. dinner) but leave compound words (e.g. football, toothbrush) until last.

4) Ask children to work out how many words there are in a particular phrase or sentence. Provide them with a number of blank cards (more than they need), say the sentence and the children must decide how many cards they need. Many children split the words into syllables at this point, but explain that you can only write whole words onto the cards.

5) Say a sentence with two words swapped around for children to correct, for example: We can cake a bake; I scratch my finger with my nose; Sweets like children. Rearranging words in this way leads to working with a sentence-maker.

Developing awareness of syllables within words

1) Split a word into syllables and say with pauses between. Can children work out what you mean? (See 'Robot Talk' in above section). Add natural intonation if children need a clue.

2) Draw a word of several syllables (e.g. elephant/computer/helicopter) and cut it into the same number of pieces using *slanted* cuts to differentiate from whole words. Place these pieces face down in the correct order, separated by gaps. Say each syllable one at a time, pointing to each piece as you speak. When children blend them seamlessly to reconstruct the word, they turn the pieces over to make the word like a jigsaw puzzle. Leave compound words (e.g. foot+ball) until last, as children often take a while to perceive the new meaning.

3) Reverse this activity by saying the whole word as you run your finger across the separated pieces, and ask children to identify the separate syllables (speak like a robot). Help children by tapping each piece of paper or clapping the syllables as you speak, and avoid syllables with dyphthongs ('sliding' vowels such as 'ear', 'our').

4) Once familiar with this visual framework, ask children to clap out the syllables in a word.

5) Encourage children to finish words (e.g.'It's a don-____?' and find a picture that represents that syllable so that patterns emerge (monkey/donkey; happy/floppy/puppy etc.).

6) Make new words or names from a collection of word pictures such as 'car', 'bee', 'toe', 'bar', 'key', 'knee', 'loo', 'sea' (Toby, Lucy, Barbie etc.). Progress to compound words such as car-park, football, toothbrush, spaceman etc.

7) Ask children to name pictures and decide if each word is made of 2, 3 or 4 parts depending on the number of claps or syllables. Identify words within words and draw pictures to help visualise and remember long or difficult words.

Developing awareness of sounds within words through blending, recognition and understanding (true 'reading readiness')

1) Link individual speech sounds to pictures/symbols and *actions* for maximum impact. Encourage children to listen to a sound and find the appropriate picture/symbol, adding the action as an extra cue as necessary. Start with the earliest range of pure speech sounds (phonemes) 'm', 'n', 'f', 's', 'sh', 'l', 'p', 't', 'c', 'k', 'b', 'd', 'g' and *long vowels*.

2) In all blending activities present children with sounds and syllables to blend, *rather than the target word*. Let children discover for themselves what word is produced when they blend the sounds together, either by their own voice-recognition, or by selecting from a small choice of pictures. Young children can again be asked to work out what the robot is trying to say.

3) In the following activities, C and V (consonant/vowel) refer to pure sounds rather than their alphabetic (phonic) equivalent, and we concentrate on how we *say* rather than *spell* words.

4) Introduce blending by turning a picture face down and saying the target word in two parts (single sound plus syllable) rather than breaking it down into sounds alone. *Do not split the word before a vowel* until children can succeed with the more natural blends: i.e. ca-**t**, for-**k**, co-**m**b, **s**-mile, **c**-lock – rather than **c**-at, **f**-ork, **c**-omb, **sm**-ile, **cl**-ock. Help by almost hovering between sound and syllable and gradually extending the gap between them. Once children produce (and hopefully recognise) the word, they turn the picture over.

5) Place a sound before/after a simple CV or CVC picture. Can children blend to discover a new word? For example, bee+**k** = beak, bell+**t** = belt, sing+**k** = sink, **s**+no = snow, **b**+loo = blue.

6) Reverse the above activity by giving children a selection of sounds (use only p, t, c/k, m, n, f, s, sh at first) and a picture of CVC or CVCC words (e.g. sheet, farm, house, knife, tent, pink, jump). For each picture say all of the word except the final consonant ('she ...', 'far ...', 'how ...', 'nigh ...', 'ten ...', 'ping ...', 'jum ...' etc.) and ask children to say or find the correct sound to finish the word.

7) Take a V or VC picture like 'eye' or 'eat' and experiment with different sounds to produce rhyme-strings (e.g. pie, lie, my, tie, shy, sheet, meat, neat, feet, seat). Reverse by saying one of the target words (e.g. pie) and ask the child to find the sound/picture combination that produced that word ('p' + 'eye').

8) Say a CVC word running your finger from left to right across the picture and ask children to identify either the *first* or *last* sound. Start with long consonants ('m', 'n', 'l', 's', 'sh', 'f') at the *beginning* of the word and 'm', 'n', 's', 'f', 'p', 't', 'k' at the *end* (these sounds can be prolonged/emphasised without distorting the word). Add the action-link as an extra cue as necessary.

9) Identifying sounds in this way leads to more traditional phonics programmes, and blending and segmenting practice with the full range of consonants and vowels.

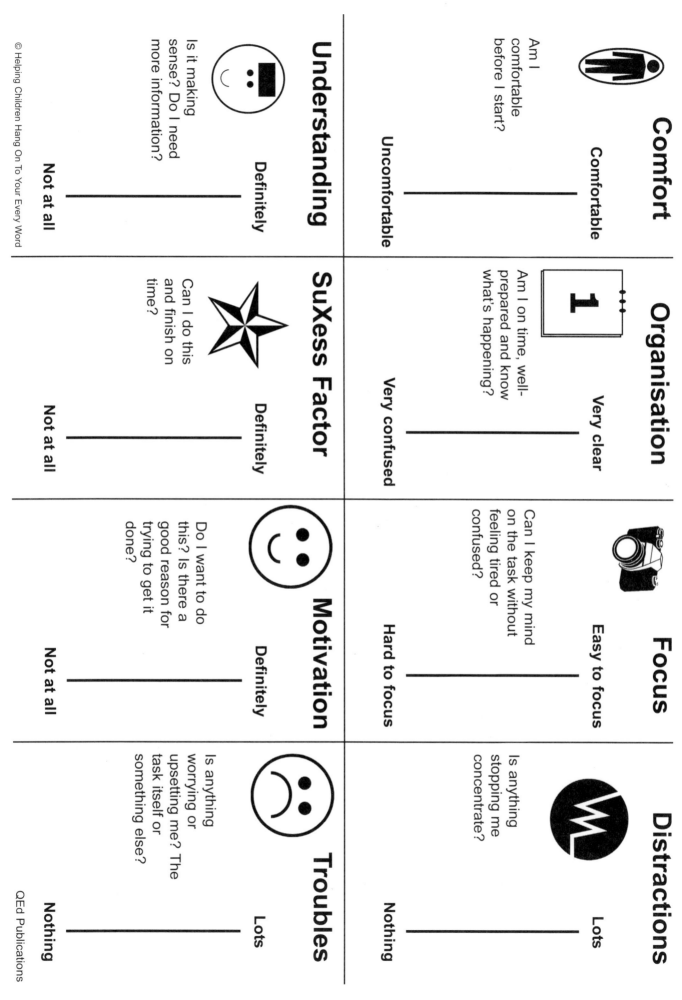

Comfort

Am I comfortable before I start?

Comfortable ———————— Uncomfortable

Organisation

Am I on time, well-prepared and know what's happening?

Very clear ———————— Very confused

Focus

Can I keep my mind on the task without feeling tired or confused?

Easy to focus ———————— Hard to focus

Understanding

Is it making sense? Do I need more information?

Definitely ———————— Not at all

SuXess Factor

Can I do this and finish on time?

Definitely ———————— Not at all

Motivation

Do I want to do this? Is there a good reason for trying to get it done?

Definitely ———————— Not at all

Distractions

Is anything stopping me concentrate?

Lots ———————— Nothing

Troubles

Is anything worrying or upsetting me? The task itself or something else?

Lots ———————— Nothing

Comfort

Am I sitting comfortably in a good position?

Can I move easily?

Are my clothes comfortable?

Is there good light?

Am I the right temperature?

Is anything hurting or disturbing me?

When did I last go to the toilet?

Organisation

Do I know . . . .
- What I have to do?
- What the teacher is looking for?
- How long it will last?
- What's happening next?

Have I got a workplan?

Have I got everything I need?

Have I put away everything I *don't* need?

Who can help if I get stuck?

Focus

Do I feel awake?

How many things do I need to think about?

Can I concentrate on them all at once?

Is it making sense?

Is it wearing me out?

Will I do better if I tackle one thing at a time?

Will I do better after a short break to move around?

Distractions

Do I know what I should be focusing on?

Do I keep looking at or listening to other things?

Can I ignore them?

Can I remove them or move away from them?

Do I keep thinking about other things?

Can I tell someone and then get on?

Understanding

Do I know what's going on?

Do I know why we're doing it?

Can I hear properly?

Can I see properly?

Do the words make sense?

Do the pictures make sense?

Is it going too fast?

Can I remember it?

Do I need more clues?

Who do I ask for help?

SuXess Factor

Can I do this?

Can I do it if I keep trying?

Have I got enough time to do it?

Have I got enough help?

Could I do just part of it?

What part could I manage?

Can I see how well I am doing?

Motivation

Am I enjoying this?

Why not?

What would make it better/easier?

How can it benefit me?

What will happen if I don't do it?

Is it worth putting off any longer?!

Troubles

Am I feeling angry or upset about anything?

Am I worrying about anything?

Am I thinking about these things most of the time?

Who could help me change things so those thoughts and feelings went away?